THE REAL READER'S QUARTERLY

Slightly Foxed

'A Great Adventure'

NO.38   SUMMER 2013

Editors Gail Pirkis and Hazel Wood
Marketing and publicity Stephanie Allen and Jennie Paterson
Subscriptions Alarys Gibson, Anna Kirk and Faith McAllister

Cover illustration: Emily Sutton, 'Country Show'

Emily Sutton is an artist and illustrator who lives and works in York. She has illustrated children's books for the Victoria and Albert Museum and Walker Books, and has worked on projects for Bettys and Taylors, Random House, Penguin Books and Hermes among others. She especially enjoys drawing interesting junk-shop finds and shop fronts. For more examples of her work see www.emillustrates.com.

Design by Octavius Murray

Layout by Andrew Evans

Colophon and tailpiece by David Eccles

© The contributors 2013

Published by Slightly Foxed Limited
53 Hoxton Square
London N1 6PB

tel 020 7033 0258
fax 0870 1991245
e-mail all@foxedquarterly.com
www.foxedquarterly.com

Slightly Foxed is published quarterly in early March, June, September and December
Annual subscription rates (4 issues)
UK £40; Europe £48; Rest of the World £52
Single copies of this issue can be bought for £10 (UK), £12 (Europe) or £13 (Rest of the World)
Back issues are also available

ISBN 978-1-906562-50-2
Printed and bound by Smith Settle, Yeadon, West Yorkshire

Contents

Ian Stephens, 'Daisies', wood engraving

Our bookshop can obtain any of the books mentioned in this issue.
Slightly Foxed on Gloucester Road, 123 Gloucester Road,
London SW7 4TE · enquiries@foxedbooks.com · tel: 020 7370 3503

From the Editors

Well, summer's here – at last. There are still plenty of people about in Hoxton Square, but it won't be long before the city starts to empty out and that particular summer quiet descends which, if you're still working, makes you feel both grateful and wistful at the same time.

Whether you're travelling or not, the latest of the Slightly Foxed Editions is, we feel, the perfect summer read. We love all our books, but *Country Boy* (see p. 14) is somehow especially close to our hearts, partly because it is such a compelling story and partly because of the modest and delightful character of its author. Richard Hillyer – whose real name was Charles Stranks – was a farm boy growing up in a remote Buckinghamshire village in the days before the First World War. There was no chance of his going to grammar school, but somehow he discovered books, and with agonizing determination taught himself Latin, finally winning a scholarship to Durham University – something unheard of then for a boy from his background. It's an account of a lost world and of a personal journey that is unsentimental yet poetic and very moving.

Come the autumn we'll be embarking on a new and exciting publishing venture. Between the 1950s and the 1970s the splendid storyteller Ronald Welch produced a series of children's books which some readers may still remember with nostalgia. Following the fortunes of the Carey family from their involvement in the Crusades to their service in the First World War, these novels are gripping reads which also provide a wonderful overview of English history. Unaccountably they've long been out of print and difficult to find, so we're delighted to be bringing them to life again in a new series,

Slightly Foxed Cubs. Read more about it on p.95 of this issue.

The *Slightly Foxed* diary is pretty full this year. On Wednesday 19 June we're off to the West Country, hosting a 'Tea with *Slightly Foxed*' at the Simonsbath Festival on Exmoor (www.simonsbathfestival.co.uk). Then on 5–7 July we'll be manning a stall at the Ways with Words Festival at Dartington Hall in Devon – a delicious setting if ever there was one. If you're planning to be there, do keep a lookout for us (www.wayswithwords.co.uk). And on Saturday 20 July we'll be at the Penzance Literary Festival for another 'Tea with *Slightly Foxed*' (www.penzance-literary-festival.org.uk).

On Saturday 9 November we'll be hosting our third Readers' Day at the Art Workers' Guild in Bloomsbury. This event has become one of the highlights of our year – a great chance to meet subscribers, and for subscribers to meet and hear some of our contributors. It's very relaxed and thoroughly enjoyable. Tony and his staff will be there with a selection of books from the shop, and, as always, tea and mouth-watering cakes will be provided by our contributor Frances Donnelly. Tickets for the day (including morning coffee and afternoon tea) cost £50 – the same as last year. They really do go like hot cakes, so if you're planning to come, do book soon.

Our older writers' competition brought in a gratifying number of entries. It was extraordinarily hard to choose a winner so we've decided to award equal honours to four: Gus Alexander, Paul Brassley, Cynthia Clinch and Donald Watson, each of whom will receive £250. You can read Cynthia Clinch's piece on the delightful-sounding children's book *The Far-Distant Oxus* on p.82, and the others will appear in *Slightly Foxed* at intervals during the coming year. It's great to find such good writers among our subscribers. Congratulations to you all.

GAIL PIRKIS

HAZEL WOOD

A Great Adventure

ANDREW MERRILLS

Few people living at the time would have regarded the early Thirties as a golden age, nor has posterity been kind to the period that W. H. Auden described as 'a low, dishonest decade'. In 1933, the Japanese invaded Manchuria, Hitler became Chancellor of the Reich, and the first stirrings of the Spanish Civil War were felt in Catalonia. While hindsight bathes 1914 in the gentle summer glow of a prelapsarian world, the early Thirties seem autumnal and telescope all too easily into the bitter winter that was to follow. But for one man at least, the cold months of 1933–4 provided a still moment in time, which he would remember with fondness for the rest of his life.

In late December 1933, Patrick Leigh Fermor set out on foot for Constantinople (as he anachronistically termed it). Recently expelled from school for the unpardonable crime of holding hands with a local girl, and insufficiently inspired by the prospect of Sandhurst and a career of peacetime soldiering, the 19-year-old decided to head east on foot. His backpack was evidently stuffed to the brim, with a great-coat, jerseys, shirts (including white linen ones for dressy occasions), puttees, nailed boots, a selection of stationery, a copy of *The Oxford Book of English Verse* and the first volume of the Loeb *Horace*. The clothing was soon lost but was replaced as he headed east by many generous donations from hosts and chance acquaintances. The litera-

Patrick Leigh Fermor, *A Time of Gifts* (1977: 304pp · £9.99 ·
ISBN 9780719566950) and *Between the Woods and the Water* (1982: 256pp ·
£9.99 · ISBN 9780719566967) are available as paperbacks from John Murray, as
is, in hardback, Artemis Cooper's biography, *Patrick Leigh Fermor: An Adventure*
(2012: 464pp · £25 · ISBN 9780719554490).

ture was a more permanent part of his baggage; though he lost his *Oxford* volume, this was complemented by a vast corpus of writing in English, French and Latin that he had committed to memory. A little over a year later, the young traveller arrived at the Golden Horn.

Writing the account of the journey would take much longer. The first of three projected volumes, *A Time of Gifts*, was published in 1977, when the author was 62; the second, *Between the Woods and the Water*, which traces the journey from the Hungarian frontier (where the first leaves off) to the Iron Gates in Romania, came in 1982. The third book remained unfinished at the time of the author's death in 2011.

Between the long adventure itself and its eventual publication, Patrick Leigh Fermor had led an improbably rich and full life. He was famous for his wartime heroism in occupied Crete, where he lived as a shepherd among the resistance fighters in the mountains and masterminded the daring abduction of the German garrison commander. These actions were commemorated in the memoir *Ill Met by Moonlight* by his colleague Sandy Moss, and his own role was played by Dirk Bogarde in the 1957 Powell and Pressburger film of the same title. In the decades that followed, Leigh Fermor produced some of the finest travel writing in English. His published books included a seminal study of the Caribbean in *The Traveller's Tree*, a reflection on the monastic life in *A Time to Keep Silence*, and two remarkable books on Greece, *Mani* and *Roumeli* (see *SF* No.2).

Much has been written about him since his death, and each of his books has its own admirers. But for those new to his writing, there is no better place to start than with *A Time of Gifts* and *Between the Woods and the Water*, as an introduction both to the young man on the brink of a great adventure, and the mature writer at the height of his powers. While both shine through in these two books, it is the former who strikes the reader most forcibly. Almost immediately, we are confronted with the extraordinary personality of the young man who wanders across their pages, and it is easy to imagine how this spirit must have charmed and delighted those with whom he came into contact.

His was a well-populated road, from the two German girls in Stuttgart who swept the young 'Mr Brown' into an exhilarating tumble of drinking, singing and Christmas parties, to the lugubrious Frisian in Vienna who shared his poverty and some ingenious schemes for generating money before disappearing into the murky world of saccharine-smuggling on the Middle Danube. And these are some of his less remarkable social successes. By the time he reached Mitteleuropa proper, Leigh Fermor had become the darling of the fading imperial aristocracy. We read of raucous games of bicycle polo on the lawns of castles, of horses borrowed for a few days' ride across the Great Hungarian Plain, and a seemingly endless succession of benevolent Anglophiles who welcomed the dusty young traveller with food, alcohol and the free run of their libraries. Even if we sometimes feel a tinge of envy at the ease with which the young Patrick drifted into this travellers' inheritance, it is hard to begrudge him it: the same easy charms that won over the inhabitants of central Europe in the 1930s can still delight a reader eighty years later.

Mark Handley   Leigh Fermor has always been loved for the richness of his prose, and both books do full justice to the deep romantic undercurrents of the rivers along which he was travelling. Yet even in his most purple passages, he has a peculiarly literary sensitivity; he writes, not as a traveller in uncharted lands, but as one who is acutely aware of the many writers who have come before him. Nor is this simply the prerogative of the adult writer, usurping the fresh observations of youth with his own literary stylizations. The wide-eyed observer at centre stage also views the world through the lens of his reading. Take this account of Wachau in *A Time of Gifts*:

> Melk was the threshold of this unspeakably beautiful valley. As we have seen by now, castles beyond counting had been loom-

ing along the river. They were perched on dizzier spurs here, more dramatic in decay and more mysteriously cobwebbed with fable. The towered headlands dropped sheer, the liquid arcs flowed round them in semicircles. From ruins further from the shore the land sloped more gently, and vineyards and orchards descended in layers to the tree-reflecting banks. The river streamed past wooded islands and when I gazed either way, the seeming water-staircase climbed into the distance. Its associations with the *Niebelungenlied* are close, but later mythology haunts it. If any landscape is the meeting place of chivalrous romance and fairy tales, it is this. The stream winds into distances where Camelot or Avalon might lie, the woods suggest mythical fauna, the songs of Minnesingers and the sound of horns just out of earshot.

If anyone was attuned to the mythic properties of Old Europe it was the knight errant of 1934. Leigh Fermor gazed at the unfolding landscape with a romantic longing inflamed by a short life stuffed with literature and history. When he passed through the Low Countries, he looked through Bruegel's eyes; his view of Vienna was a palimpsest of Ottoman armies and Habsburg emperors, against which the complex realities of the mid-1930s were not always visible to him. And when not prompted into reverie by the landscapes around him, he turned inward to the rich body of literature that he had committed to memory. The list of these works is among the most famous passages of Leigh Fermor's writing. I won't cite it in full here, since it runs to several pages, but it includes (among *many* other things) Shakespeare, Spenser, Keats, 'an abundance of A. E. Housman', the Sitwells, Norman Douglas and Evelyn Waugh, 'large quantities of Villon', and a respectable body of Virgil, Horace, Catullus and Lucan.

If a love of literature brightened the colours of Leigh Fermor's world, it also created a deeper yearning, and this is perhaps his most appealing trait, at least to me. Time and again, he writes of the fervour with which he engaged in spirited conversation with his learned hosts or plunged himself into their well-furnished libraries. Here, he gulped great draughts of European history, poring over details of Germanic folklore or piecing together the complex literary heritage of the world through which he was passing, and which was soon to be lost forever. In recounting these moments, his prose reaches its sublime best, as when he talks about the libraries of Prague:

> Where, in this half-recollected maze, do the reviving memories of the libraries belong? To the Old University, perhaps, one of the most ancient and famous in Europe, founded by the great King Charles IV in 1384. I'm not sure. But I drive wedge-shaped salients into oblivion nevertheless and follow them through the recoiling mists with enfilading perspectives of books until bay after bay coheres. Each of them is tiered with burnished leather bindings and gold and scarlet gleam on the spines of hazel and chestnut and pale vellum. Globes space out the chessboard floors. There are glass-topped homes for incunables. Triangular lecterns display graduals and antiphonals and Books of Hours and coloured scenes encrust the capitals on the buckled parchment; block-notes and lozenges climb and fall on four-letter Georgian staves where Carolingian uncials and blackletter spell out the responses. The concerted spin of a score of barley-sugar pillars uphold elliptic galleries where brass combines with polished oak, and obelisks and pineapples alternate on the balustrades.

The conceit which underscores this passage – the image of memory as a library – is a key theme throughout both books. Not only does this recall the prodigious literary memory of the young man, it also reminds us of the act of memory that went into the composition of the books themselves. While *A Time of Gifts* and *Between the Woods and the Water* do an exquisite job in representing the world through the eyes of a 19-year-old, the reader never forgets the mature writer who acts as mediator and amanuensis. For the successful travel writer, war hero and beloved raconteur who wrote these books, these are stories of a half-remembered youth as well as a half-forgotten Europe.

'For now the time of gifts is gone' runs the line from Louis MacNeice that provides Leigh Fermor's first title, and it is this faint melancholy which makes both books so powerful. These are the memories of a lifetime, and in writing them down, in revisiting the notebooks and the maps that had lain untouched for years, the writer creates them anew. Nowhere is this more apparent than in the conclusion to the most intimate episode of the sequence. For a giddy chapter, the traveller had careered around Transylvania in a car with his close friend István, and with Angéla, something of a kindred spirit. The reader is caught up in the breathless pleasure of the episode, which climaxes in a manic motor chase with a west-bound train, but which deflates as the companions consider their parting:

> The reader may think that I am lingering too long over these pages. I think so too, and I know why: when we reached our destination in an hour or two, we would have come full cycle. It wasn't only an architectural world, but the whole sequence of these enchanted Transylvanian months that would come to a stop. I was about to turn south, away from all my friends, and the dactylic ring of Magyar would die away. Then there was István; I would miss him bitterly; and the loss of Angéla – who is little more than a darting luminous phantom in these pages – would be a break I could hardly bear to think of; and I can't help putting off the moment for a paragraph or two.

Everyone has their favourite sections of these extraordinary books, whether they are drinking songs in snow-bound Germany, the majestic descriptions of pre-war Vienna, or the madcap charabanc rides through Transylvania. Mine comes at the beginning of the narrative.

The account of the Groote Kirk in Rotterdam isn't as succulent as some of the richer morsels later on – the young traveller had only just entered the continent, and both he and his older self were keen to get on. But it captures the themes of the book perfectly:

> Filled with dim early morning light, the concavity of grey masonry and whitewash joined in pointed arches high overhead and the floor diminished along the nave in a chessboard of black and white flagstones. So compellingly did the vision tally with a score of half-forgotten Dutch pictures that my mind's eye instantaneously furnished the void with those seventeenth-century groups which should have been sitting or strolling there: burghers with pointed corn-coloured beards – and impious spaniels that refused to stay outside – conferring gravely with their wives and children, still as chessmen, in black broadcloth and identical honeycomb ruffs under the tremendous hatchmented pillars. Except for this church, the beautiful city was to be bombed to fragments a few years later. I would have lingered, had I known.

'I would have lingered, had I known': these are books for readers, for poets and for travellers. But most of all, they're books for lingerers.

ANDREW MERRILLS is a lecturer in Ancient History. He likes walking, Latin poetry and the thought of madcap charabanc rides through Transylvania, but has yet to combine them in a single holiday.

B. Lodge

Immemorial Rhythm

GORDON BOWKER

It's human nature perhaps to look back on our early years as a time of enchantment. Kenneth Grahame, Angela Thirkell and Laurie Lee, among others, have all attempted to recapture the 'golden age' of their childhood. My own golden age was spent in a picturesque village on the banks of the River Dart. Most villagers then were from old Devon families of farmers and fishermen whose ancestors' gravestones in the churchyard stood witness to their antiquity. The oldest church chorister and chief bell-ringer had been singing and ringing there since Victorian times. Over surrounding hillsides, horse-drawn ploughs turned green fields into patches of deep red earth each September, and along the lanes at evening the ploughman still did 'homeward plod his weary way'.

Time lends such memories a nostalgic glow, but few have recalled that now distant rural way of life with such riveting honesty as Richard Hillyer in his memoir *Country Boy*. Richard Hillyer was the pseudonym used by Charles James Stranks, the son of a poor farm labourer, born at the dawn of the last century in the isolated Buckinghamshire village of Hardwick (here called Byfield). It was a village unchanged since Saxon times, where work was governed by the 'immemorial rhythm' of the seasons and social life revolved mostly around church and chapel and cricket pitch. It was an essentially feudal world in which the lives of the poor were dictated by the various local gentry.

Hillyer sets out to recapture a way of life which, after the Great War, had begun to disappear and was gradually fading from memory. However, his aim is more than that of mere fond recall. He wants to rescue the old English village from those who, like Hardy, offered a middle-class intellectual view of rural life, and romanticists who saw the countryside either as a place of quaint customs and ancient ways or a 'cesspit of strange iniquities peopled . . . with sadists and psychopaths'. He portrays with unflinching reality the squalor and misery of village life before the First World War, where impoverished labourers were often at the mercy of cruel and heartless farmers. Yet though his writing is unsentimental it is also wonderfully poetic, for he recaptures the magic of that remote countryside, and the effect it had on the imagination of a sensitive and highly intelligent boy with few outlets for his feelings and no one to share his interests.

For Hillyer, the impoverished labourers among whom he grew up, descendants of the old English peasantry, are the real creators of the village's character and guardians of its traditions, and it is their powers of endurance, 'courage, wisdom and sly humour' which have enabled them to survive. In old Byfield, the social order is unchangeable – everyone knows his or her place and all leave this life no better off than when they entered it. Above the Hillyers stand the Rector Mr Driffield, the Minister of the chapel Mr Bilbee, and the schoolmaster Mr Wickens, while on the very top of the heap sits the wealthy owner of Byfield House, Mr du Cane, and the Squire, Lord Postern, to whom all are expected to defer.

[Lord Postern] would call at a cottage or two . . . not getting off his horse, but thumping with his hunting crop on the door . . . until somebody came out. Generally it was a woman . . . and she would stand in the doorway with her hands respectfully hidden under her apron, hardly daring to answer his questions with more than a plain, 'Yes, my Lord,' or 'No, my Lord.' 'Tell your husband his potatoes are looking well.' 'Yes, my Lord.' 'These your children?' nodding toward any that might have followed their mother to the door . . . 'Yes, my Lord.' 'Well good day to you, good day.' A touch with the crop, and the mare would move on to another.

At the very bottom lies the wretched figure of the reclusive outcast Barky Britnell, exploited and terrorized since childhood by cruel local farmers and taunted by wanton village boys.

When [Barky] flew into one of his rages he just made hoarse, strangled sounds like a tormented animal. Some lout, who had worked him up and was enjoying the fun, showing off before other grinning louts one day, said, 'He is like a dog. Listen to him barking. Barky Britnell!' And so Barky he was.

Poor Barky's cabin is squalid beyond belief – 'a one-storeyed hut' lit by three small windows, with no fire-grate and peeling walls 'showing the yellow clay underneath festering like a sore'.

But life in Hillyer's Byfield is not all wretchedness. Blazing summer days for the children mean bathing in the village pond, and Richard recalls 'the full, rich, sensual pleasure of lying naked on the short grass, until the skin was dry, and prickly with heat, and then to plunge down into the quiet depths of the pool, among the long, smooth water-lily roots that caressed the body in passing like delicate fingers'.

And there is the annual flower show in the Rectory garden, with fruit and vegetable competitions, where everybody turns out in their Sunday best for the judging, and there is dancing on the lawn to a band hired by the Rector.

Richard's immediate family – father, mother and brother John –

exist on 15 shillings a week, so for them life is frugal in the extreme. In the evening, the children's supper consists of two slices of bread and dripping and a cup of cold water. Their future looks bleak. Richard, as the son of a poor labourer, can expect little more than a life crushed beneath 'the suffocating weight of endless toil'.

But this is a story of metamorphosis, of success against the heaviest odds. Richard is a bright, attentive schoolboy eager to learn. From passages of Ben Jonson, Tennyson, Dickens and the Bible which are randomly handed out in class, he discovers the magic of language that opens doors to worlds unimagined. Soon he is reading any book he can find, and Mr Wickens hints at a place at the grammar school. But hopes raised are quickly dashed. His parents could never afford the fees.

Even so, his hunger for learning remains insatiable. Salvaging an old copy of Scott's *Waverley* discarded for burning he starts a library, and the discovery of a second-hand bookstall in Billington, the nearby market town, adds poetry and classics to his collection. Then, when a prosperous uncle from Canada dies, there is hope of an inheritance which will both alleviate the family's poverty and help Richard to the grammar school. But everything goes to Mr Hillyer's sister, and the disappointment is unbearable.

So Richard is sent to work on a local farm and arrives just in time for haymaking.

When the mowing stopped, and the horses were turned out to graze, everybody set to work to turn over yesterday's cutting. Men and boys moved in a line, each a step or two behind the other, backwards and forwards across the field at a quick walk, turning the swathe, with a deft touch of the rake, in an unbroken ribbon. It was hard to keep up at first, but as the knack grew and the movements became familiar, there was something soothing in it. All day there were the changing scents of the hayfield. The raw smell of the fresh grass in the morning, the honey smell of clover, the earthy dampness of the underside as the rakes exposed the long lines of drying grass to the sun, the sweet, dry perfume of the hay that was loaded in the evening; all of it unique, primeval, satisfying.

It was tough, backbreaking work, yet 'I was happy in a new experience,' he writes, 'something had been added to the delight of life.' In the same way the writer in him glories in the silence of the dawn as he makes his way towards the farm to do the milking:

There has been rain in the night, and the last leaves that still cling to the bushes hang wet and dejected. It is just growing light enough to see that they are there . . . In front of me the path, without footsteps to mark it since the rain fell, looks bright and new; even the muddy places have been flattened out, and catch what light there is on their wet surfaces. For the five minutes that it takes to walk to work I am alone, in a friendly world.

For Richard the life of learning now seems to be well out of reach, but he is not discouraged. From old schoolbooks he begins to teach himself Latin, and he so astonishes the Rector with his knowledge that he is offered coaching and the prospect of sitting for a scholarship to Durham University.

Meanwhile Byfield is undergoing change. Lloyd George's old age pension brings hope to poor parishioners, and 'The Kaiser's War' further disturbs the settled order. Richard's brother John and the local farm-horses depart for France, villagers are directed into factory work, and soldiers from the industrial north are stationed in Byfield.

Then there are portents of a new, less leisurely age. The horse-drawn van, which once trundled the road to Billington slowly enough for passengers to study wildlife along the hedges, is replaced by an old gas-fuelled London bus which rattles along at speed. In a new age of travel, the old Byfield which 'imprisoned and consumed its own children' will slowly disappear.

Richard Hillyer recaptures the lost world of an old English village with realism and compassion. He depicts the villagers of Byfield with the caring eye of a Zola or a Van Gogh, lost souls resurrected – the lowly ploughman, the wretched outcast, the village schoolmaster, the pedlar, the women worn down by hopeless poverty. Hillyer is their camera, their quiet observer.

Eventually, thanks to the Rector, young Richard does manage to escape, winning a scholarship to Durham University. From the minute he first sees the city, with its great cathedral – 'that wonder among buildings' – rising above the winding medieval streets, Durham seems to have been his spiritual home. It represented everything he had longed for, cultivation and refinement and the rich life of the mind from which he had so long been excluded. When he receives the news of his scholarship we, like him, can hardly believe he has done it, the odds stacked against him were so great.

Searches have revealed little about the later life of this fascinating man, apart from the fact that he wrote a good many books, mainly on ecclesiastical subjects, and became a canon of Durham Cathedral. But in his youth we come to know him intimately. There can be few more painfully honest and moving accounts of growing up poor than *Country Boy*. It is not only a fine piece of social history, but a cliffhanger that keeps one gripped right to the end.

GORDON BOWKER has written four literary biographies – of Malcolm Lowry, Lawrence Durrell, George Orwell and James Joyce.

Richard Hillyer's *Country Boy* (256pp) is now available from *Slightly Foxed* in a new limited and numbered cloth-bound pocket edition of 2,000 copies, each priced at £16 (UK), £18 (Europe) or £19 (Rest of the World). All prices include post and packing. Copies may be ordered by post (53 Hoxton Square, London N1 6PB), by phone (020 7033 0258) or via our website www.foxedquarterly.com.

Holden Revisited

YSENDA MAXTONE GRAHAM

Two photographs exist of me reading *The Catcher in the Rye*. One was taken thirty years ago by my father, on the top bunk bed in a sleeper train bound for Edinburgh. I was 19. The book was the orange Penguin edition, which I'd recently bought in Cambridge market.

The other was taken by my husband in December 2011, at home in London. I was 48, on the sofa with the dog. The book was the very same Cambridge market paperback, my maiden name in neat handwriting in the top right-hand corner of the pre-title page.

To read that book aged 19 and aged 48 is to read it in two quite different ways. As I reread it last year, moved to tears by its poignancy, I tried to relive the experience of reading it for the first time thirty years ago. What was that chubby-cheeked undergraduate's reaction as she got to know Holden Caulfield while passing through Doncaster, York and Northallerton?

I think she was thinking how cool it all was. How cool *I* was to be reading this coolest of books!

If you really want to hear about it, the first thing you'll probably want to know is where I was born, and what my lousy childhood was like, and how my parents were occupied and all before they had me, and all that David Copperfield kind of crap, but I don't feel like going into it.

J. D. Salinger, *The Catcher in the Rye* (1951)
Penguin · Pb · 192pp · £8.99 · ISBN 9780140237504

So nonchalant and depressive was the narrator's tone, from the very first sentence, that I think I subconsciously adopted a corresponding gum-chewing facial expression while reading. The very fact that the narrator didn't 'feel like going into it' made me ache to find out. He had refused to proffer any information, and had done so in a bored way, yet I was gripped.

My parents would have about two haemorrhages apiece if I told anything pretty personal about them.

And so flippant about his parents! So immediate, so direct was the narrator's voice that it felt as if Holden Caulfield himself was talking to me. I half-forgot that there was a 32-year-old middleman, namely J. D. Salinger, recreating my generation's voice and way of thinking.

Here was a 17-year-old who just walked out of his private school late one night and took a train to New York. He took cabs, he drank whisky, he chain-smoked, he even called up a prostitute; he was alone against the world, a solitary rebel in New York in the night, spending dollars and dimes. The Edward Hopper exhibition had come to London in 1980, and I was still full of it in 1982. 'It was so quiet and so lonesome out, even though it was Saturday night. I didn't see hardly anybody on the street.'

Mark Handley

Reading sentences like that, I was in a Hopper painting, and wallowing in it. Bring on the gloom! I lived through Holden's sleepless three-day adventure, minute by minute, relishing the slow descent into despair. I didn't cry. The act of reading it without crying was a reinforcement of my maturity; a kind of bravado. 'Lay it on thick: I can take it!' Holden's story seemed hypothetical. Direct though his voice was, I still experienced him as a literary figure rather than a replica of a real one.

But, reading the book again aged 48, I went through two handkerchiefs. In those thirty years, I had met or heard about real people who had more than a whiff of Holden Caulfield about them – and not the glamour whiff, the despair whiff. The whole thing seemed appallingly real and possible.

And this time, I wasn't Holden Caulfield. I was his mother. 'For God's sake, get some sleep!' I wanted to yell at Holden. 'Stop smoking! Stop drinking! You need a square meal. I hope you remembered to bring some condoms, young man. Stop wasting *our* money on taxis! And when did you last brush your teeth?'

But as well as having this brisk, practical, motherly reaction, I felt raw pain while reading the book – far more pain than I'd felt the first time. Then, Holden had seemed mature, manly and full of 'street cred' as I called it, describing things like his double-dating experience in Ed Banky's car. Now he seemed innocent, guileless, childlike in many ways, hopelessly unready for the pitiless ways of the adult world. Yes, he drinks whiskies; but in some of the bars he goes into he's seen as a 'minor' and is only allowed Coke. When I read that thirty years ago, I thought, 'God, how petty and authoritarian!' Now, I saw this as an emblem of Holden's being in that uncomfortable, awkward period between being a child and being an adult.

He never thinks further ahead than the next hour. This teenage short-termism is familiar to me now as a parent; it exasperates me, but it saddens me too. Reading Holden's narrative, you see just how such a directionless and solitary descent into misery could happen.

> The first thing I did when I got off at Penn Station, I went into this phone booth. I felt like giving somebody a buzz. I left my bags right outside the booth so that I could watch them, but as soon as I was inside, I couldn't think of anybody to call up.

So he gets into a cab and goes to a hotel, and calls up a girl he's never met who doesn't want to see him, and goes down to the bar and tries to make friends with three girls who dance with him but don't talk to him. Then he goes on to a nightclub, packed 'mostly with prep-school jerks and college jerks', where he drinks a Scotch and soda on his own, then walks 42 blocks back to the hotel, and then the elevator man offers to bring a call-girl up to his room, 'five bucks a throw, fifteen bucks till noon'. Holden says yes, and the girl arrives in his room, but he just can't go through with the sex, he just doesn't feel like it, and the girl gets furious with him, and demands ten bucks, but he pays her five, as agreed, and then the elevator man comes back into the room, demands another five bucks, and beats Holden up.

This is the adult world at its most pitiless. The linear narrative reflects with terrifying precision the blind alleys of instant gratification. Holden has no idea what he really wants, all he feels is a vague disgust for the phoniness of everything around him, coupled with profound loneliness and undirected sexual longing.

Far from wallowing in the bleakness as I did the first time, this time I searched desperately for shafts of light. Is there no kindred spirit in the world for Holden? As in an Evelyn Waugh novel, the central character seems too fine for the coarse world around him. Cruelly, such fineness is a magnet for horrible experiences: the coarse can't resist preying on the fine.

Holden's school room-mate at Pencey, the brutish Stradlater, asks him to write his descriptive essay for him while he goes out on a date. Holden obliges him, writing an essay about the baseball mitt which belonged to his brother Allie, who died. Stradlater returns from the date. 'For Chrissake, Holden. This is about a goddam baseball glove.' After a few more 'goddams' (someone has counted; there are 238 'goddams' in the book), Holden snatches the essay out of Stradlater's hand and tears it into pieces.

And who has Stradlater been having a date with? (Or 'giving the time to', as Holden puts it.) With one of the book's two shafts of light. That is, with one of the two characters with some of Holden's sweetness and fineness about them. We never meet Jane Gallagher, but Holden describes her charm and prettiness with his typical outpouring of seemingly un-thought-out words which actually say it all. The thought that Stradlater has been 'giving the time to' Jane is part of what drives Holden's raging, mindless, self-destructive actions over the next 72 hours. It's partly jealousy, partly horror at the thought of Stradlater having his wicked way with this good and sensitive girl.

But at least the 48-year-old reading mother knows that, in this world of phoneys and aliens who respond to Holden's questions by saying 'Whatdja mean?' there is someone in the world whom Holden likes and connects with, and who likes him back, even though she might choose to go on a date with boorish Stradlater instead.

The other shaft of light is Holden's kid sister Phoebe. We meet her when Holden at last goes home (thank God), stealing into the apartment in the middle of the night hoping not to be overheard by his parents or by the maid.

> I even held my breath, for God's sake. You can hit my father over the head with a chair and he won't wake up, but my mother, all you have to do to my mother is cough somewhere in Siberia and she'll hear you. She's nervous as hell. Half the time she's up all night smoking cigarettes.

Holden finds Phoebe asleep in their absent big brother's bed; and again, with a few verbal brushstrokes he makes us care about her.

> She likes to sleep in D. B.'s room when he's away, and he lets her. You ought to see her doing her homework or something at that crazy desk of his. It's almost as big as the bed. You can hardly see her when she's doing her homework. That's the kind of stuff she likes, though. She doesn't like her own room because it's too little, she says. She says she likes to spread out. That kills me. What's old Phoebe got to spread out? Nothing.

Phoebe rightly guesses that Holden has been kicked out of Pencey, and her reaction is, 'Daddy'll kill you. Daddy's gonna kill you.' They have a *sotto voce* argument there and then, but it's shot through with love and mutual understanding. Phoebe turns away in fury, but 'I knew from the back of her neck that she was listening to me.'

And when Holden decides to run away from New York and start a new life and never come back, Phoebe tries to come with him, lugging her suitcases, and he decides not to go after all, because he doesn't want her to miss her school play. The book ends with him watching her on a merry-go-round at the zoo.

I felt so damn happy all of a sudden, the way old Phoebe kept going round and round and round.

Actually, there's one more extremely short chapter written the following year from a psychiatric institution. But that doesn't blot out the shaft of light.

I now see that Salinger's craft in recreating Holden's way of thinking and talking is superb – an astonishingly accurate concoction of a 17-year-old's haphazard thoughts and actions. More aware of the adult author's reconstructive craft, I found the book much funnier this time. At the end of a paragraph about a schoolmate's filthy, mossy teeth, his revolting way of eating mashed potatoes, his pimples and his terrible personality, comes the short sentence, 'I wasn't too crazy about him, to be honest.' Salinger is good at bathetic last sentences.

So, what about that mother of Holden's who's 'up all night smoking cigarettes'? What can we find out about her, or about Holden's father? Nothing much, except that he is some kind of 'hot-shot lawyer' and she is 'nervous as hell'. Reading *The Catcher in the Rye* aged 19, I was quite unmoved by the sense of alienation between Holden and his parents, and by the fact that he hardly mentioned them. On this latest reading my antennae were up for any data on the parents and where it had all gone wrong.

Does this mean that we need our relationship with our children more than they need their relationship with us? I fear that it does.

Though not a nervous wreck like Holden Caulfield's mother, who's 'up all night smoking cigarettes', YSENDA MAXTONE GRAHAM does suffer from bouts of sleeplessness. Her short hymn to this condition, *An Insomniac's Guide to the Small Hours*, was published last year.

The Rise of Appleby

PAUL ATTERBURY

At various stages in my life I have succumbed to the lure of crime fiction, and I have always been a habitué of second-hand bookshops. That was how I came across Michael Innes in the late 1970s, when I bought one of his books in a green Penguin edition. I read it rapidly, instantly loved it and persuaded my wife to read it. From that moment we were Innes addicts.

In the mid-1980s that marriage ended, and the shelf of Innes books disappeared. But some years later, in another second-hand shop, I found a stack of hardback crime novels in their original bright yellow Gollancz jackets. Among them was *Appleby's End* (1945) by Michael Innes. And so I began a new collection of the Appleby novels.

Michael Innes was the pseudonym of John Innes Mackintosh Stewart. He was born near Edinburgh in 1906 and went up to Oriel College, Oxford, where he read English and knew Auden and Isherwood. After graduating in 1929, he studied Freudian analysis in Vienna, and then took up a lectureship at Leeds before moving to Australia in 1936 to become Jury Professor of English Literature at the University of Adelaide. It was on the long sea voyage out from Liverpool that Stewart wrote his first mystery story, *Death at the President's Lodging* (1936), a book that both launched his career as the crime writer Michael Innes and introduced his most famous creation, Detective Inspector John Appleby.

Many of Michael Innes's 32 Inspector Appleby novels have been reissued in paperback by the House of Stratus, including *Death at the President's Lodging* (256pp · £7.99 · ISBN 9781842327326) and *Appleby's End* (216pp · £7.99 · ISBN 9781842327166).

Stewart returned to Britain after the Second World War to take up a post at Queen's University, Belfast, then moved to Christ Church, Oxford, where he eventually became Reader in English Literature and then, on retirement, Professor Emeritus. He died in 1994. Throughout this illustrious career, in addition to works on Montaigne, James Joyce, Thomas Love Peacock, Kipling, Conrad and Thomas Hardy, he wrote fifty crime novels as well as various other works of fiction, short stories and an autobiography.

John Appleby is a detective inspector when he first appears in *Death at the President's Lodging*, but in the ensuing thirty-one novels he enjoys a meteoric rise through the ranks to become Commissioner of the Metropolitan Police – and he acquires a knighthood along the way. At one point he retires and then reappears in a more senior position. His changes in rank are not always consistent but his character throughout remains the same – a well-mannered, highly educated and entertaining policeman who scatters his conversation with literary, and especially poetic, references and who relies on instinct rather than police procedure to solve cases. He is the classic intellectual detective, in some ways a forerunner of Morse and Adam Dalgleish, but without the testy intolerance of the former and the angst of the latter, and much more relaxed in his handling of suspects and of the cases that Innes throws at him.

The jacket of my Gollancz edition of *Appleby's End*, the tenth in the series, includes a short quotation from an *Illustrated London News* book critic: 'Quite crazy, lavishly ingenious and extremely good fun'. It is all of that, and much more. The setting is southern England immediately after the Second World War, and the book starts with a railway journey through a landscape where nothing quite works and ancient trains clank along almost forgotten branch lines. It is winter and snow is falling.

Sunday afternoon, which in England subtly spreads itself even over the face of inanimate nature, stretched to the horizon. The fields were clothed in patchy white like half-hearted penitents; here and there cattle stood steamy and dejected, burdened like their fellows in Thomas Hardy's poems with some intuitive low-down on essential despair; and now on the outskirts of a village the train trundled past a yellow brick conventicle constructed on the basis of hardly more cheery theological convictions. Inside the carriage it was cold and beginning to be fuggy as well. The focus of attention was a large glass bowl rather like those used in cemeteries to protect artificial flowers, but here pendulous from the roof and sheltering gas burners of a type judged moderately progressive at the Great Exhibition of 1851. Flanking this were luggage racks of a breadth nicely calculated to cause chronic anxiety in those below.

Slowly the interminable journey descends into chaos. A series of bizarre, even grotesque, passengers enter the compartment, all of whom turn out to be members of the same family, the Ravens. Having missed his connection and with nowhere to stay on an increasingly wild night, Appleby is encouraged by his travelling companions to leave the train and accept their hospitality.

In due course the train is exchanged for an antique and decrepit horse-drawn vehicle which gets stuck in a flooded river and is then carried away by the speeding torrent, along with John Appleby and Judith Raven, a young and personable sculptress.

After more adventures, including a night in a haystack, John and Judith become engaged. We never really know why Appleby was on the train in the first place but it hardly matters for he is from that moment swept up in a series of strange local goings-on which include vanishing pigs, animals turned to stone, secret marriages, strange thefts and apparent murders, some of which seem to have been predicted in stories written years ago by another member of the Raven family.

It is an entertaining adventure, but also a picture of Britain on the cusp of social change, a time when traditional ways and attitudes were increasingly being challenged by the emerging new orders of the post-war world. Strange customs, oddly named characters (a Michael Innes trait), and absurd and extravagant situations seem to combine to pitch the story to the edge of farce, but somehow it never quite falls over the precipice. Innes's hand on the tiller is always firm, even though the course being followed is not always clear. In the end, which really only becomes clear in the final paragraph, John and Judith are married, starting a new strand for future books that leads eventually to their son Bobby taking over some of the sleuthing. So despite its title, *Appleby's End* also marks a beginning.

Though little enjoyed today, Innes is one of the great names from a golden age in British crime fiction, when imaginative and convoluted plots, interesting characters and a highly literate prose style were de rigueur, along with civilized, well-spoken and intelligent detectives who took it for granted that their frequent literary, historical and artistic allusions would be understood. This age may have passed, but its legacy is still there to be enjoyed.

During the upheavals that followed a recent move, I rediscovered my copy of *Appleby's End*, still in its original, though now rather torn, yellow Gollancz jacket. I reread it at once, and all the old pleasure and excitement came flooding back. It was still, as the reviewer had said in 1945, crazy, ingenious and extremely good fun. Then I dug out my green Penguin copy of *Death at the President's Lodging*, to enjoy once more John Appleby's first appearance, the Oxford college setting, the Shakespearean references, and the complexities of a still almost incomprehensible plot. They don't make them like that any more.

PAUL ATTERBURY lives in Dorset, where he spends far too much of his time writing books about railways. When not thus engaged, he appears on the BBC's *Antiques Roadshow*.

Mastering the Mutiny

PATRICK MERCER

When John Masters' *Nightrunners of Bengal* was first published in 1951, John Raymond in the *Sunday Times* described it as 'the best historical novel about the Indian Mutiny that I have ever read'. In my view he's right, although the power of the writing makes the subject matter almost irrelevant. As it is, the author has chosen one of the most chaotic and brutal episodes in the history of the British Empire in which to set his story – and he more than does it justice. It's one of those novels that, once picked up, is almost impossible to put down. I've reread it many times and it still leaves me in a cold sweat of fear. It's an old-fashioned book, written in an old-fashioned way, and it expresses old-fashioned values.

Masters' family had served in India for several generations and he clearly draws on his forebears' experience in telling his story. Rodney Savage is an officer in the Honourable East India Company's Bengal Army, stationed in the fictional town of Bhowani (in reality the capital of the princely state of Jhansi). The book opens in the tranquil heat of a peaceful summer in a garrison town. Here an isolated European community lives side by side with sepoys of a native regiment and Indian princelings, and here the minor domestic troubles of the memsahibs and their children, and the petty envies and jealousies of mid-Victorian life are played out – the whole set against the tensions and frictions of the Indian community.

I love the texture and tempo of the writing. Unlike many modern

John Masters, *Nightrunners of Bengal* (1951), is out of print.

novelists, Masters takes almost a quarter of the book to build up a picture of fear and unhappiness concealed by the apparently happy relationship between Indian soldiers and white officers. The pace is gentle, but there are hints of impending horror. The annual regimental garden party is about to take place, and Rodney Savage supervises the building of sideshows and amusements. In previous years the sepoys have always worked contentedly, delighting in the knowledge that their efforts will please the children of the European officers. Now, however, something is wrong – the men are sulky and uncooperative.

Savage's shock at his men's truculence is beautifully drawn. The tension builds as it is revealed that chapattis carried by terrified runners, who are ignorant of their hidden message, have been intercepted by the intelligence department, and that pieces of meat are being passed from hand to hand: 'Three pieces of goat's flesh, with the skin still on them and the hair and outer layers scraped off, so that they're shining white on one side and raw red flesh on the other. One piece is always large, one a little smaller, and the other very small.' They are a code for the white men, women and children who are to be butchered, just as the goats have been.

Savage himself speaks the local language fluently and understands local customs. So he is able to talk freely to everyone and to grasp better than any of his contemporaries why the rumours of the overthrow of the British may turn into reality. He also has a complex relationship with the mystic Silver Guru – a former British soldier who has gone native and become a soothsayer.

In fact, Jhansi was a long way from the main centres of the rebellion when it broke out in June 1857, first at Meerut and then in towns across the northern Gangetic plain and central India. The Europeans in Jhansi thought their isolation from the roiling horror of the blood-letting in places such as Lucknow and Cawnpore would be their salvation. So they were taken completely by surprise when the 12th Bengal Native Infantry rose up against its officers and ritually slaughtered almost every man, woman and child. Indeed, the killings in Jhansi became a byword for treachery in Victorian society, and the well down which the murdered bodies were thrown was carefully preserved after the Mutiny had been suppressed.

Masters perfectly captures that sense of shock. Certainly, there have been hints of trouble from some of the more outspoken sepoys, but nothing that can't be sorted out – or so the British think. However, when a fire is deliberately started in the soldiers' lines and the white officers rush to take control, matters soon take a very different turn. The commanding officer Colonel Bulstrode can't understand what's amiss: he calls out to the men of his regiment by name.

Rodney had never seen sepoys behave so stupidly. They turned their heads this way and that, as if looking for somebody; their faces shone in the irregular glare, and were dark and frightened. They had become strangers, Hottentots, and there was no way of making contact with them.

Masters conveys the increasing dismay of the officers as they see their faithful, trusted men turning into monsters.

All the 88th were firing – the sepoys in the crowd and the sepoys on the guardroom veranda . . . He saw a naik shoot Colonel Bulstrode in the back. A spatter of shots struck Cornet Jimmy Waugh, and he knelt down and died. A scarlet octopus of arms pulled Max Bell off the veranda. The arms rose and fell, the bayonets flashed. Others fired in the air; all shouted an incoherent crazy chant.

Then, as mass lunacy takes hold, the whole pace of the story changes. Ordered, regimented life turns into mayhem as Savage's unloved wife is bludgeoned to death in front of him and he flees with his injured baby son in his arms. All trust has gone. Savage can depend upon no one. Who are his friends and who are now his

Daniel Macklin

enemies? At his side is Caroline Langford, the rebellious belle of bungalow life after whom he has long lusted, but there's an even more interesting contradiction in his other companion. Piroo is neither sepoy nor servant. He is the ageing regimental carpenter who on several occasions saves Savage's life. But he is also a Thug, a member of an organized gang of assassins who murder their victims by strangling them with a noose. The irony is that Savage's father had dedicated himself to ridding the country of these murderers.

The descriptions of violence jump out with stark simplicity, and here it seems clear that Masters has drawn on his own experiences in Burma in the Second World War. Bullet, bayonet and rifle butt perforate flesh and crunch bone with bloody abandon. But the novel goes much deeper than simple blood and guts, for Masters' characterization is spellbinding. One of the great figures of the Mutiny was the Rani of Jhansi, a brave and beautiful she-warrior who is still an icon in India today, for she was one of the very few rulers who emerged from that period with her honour intact. Imaginary Bhowani has the same woman at its head and Savage has a complicated relationship with her: we never quite know if she's at his throat or at his feet. One moment she seems ready to become Savage's mistress: 'she opened her arms, stumbled forward and pressed her wet body against him'; while in the next paragraph, she springs back, 'eyes glittering, lips spitting', and raises a pistol to shoot him. It's compelling stuff, a heady cocktail of lust and danger.

The bloodshed, the sheer horror of events as formerly trustworthy men turn on their officers drives Savage to the brink of madness. Again, I'm sure this is drawn from life, for Masters witnessed some of the most harrowing episodes of the war against Japan where the fighting was bitter and frequently at very close quarters. At the start of the tale, Savage is noble, compassionate, a natural leader who is loved by his men. But the brutality makes him feral – he kills and kills again, and only Caroline's humanity saves him from becoming as bad as the blood-drunk mutineers. Masters knows all about fear – his descriptions make the hairs stand up on the back of your neck.

Surprisingly, there are some inaccuracies in the book. A handful of dates are wrong and there is the odd technical slip. And Masters writes about the casual racism of the time with a candour that would be unacceptable today. But neither of these aspects diminishes the skill of the writing.

I love this period. It's an epoch that's now neglected, often buried by revisionist thinking, but one in which so much happened to change British attitudes in India that it deserves to be written about more. John Masters knows how to make his pen charge and how to make it walk; he knows how to make his readers leap to attention and when to let them stand easy. And, undoubtedly, he is at his best when translating his own experiences into those of his hero. Read this and sweat; read this and understand fear.

PATRICK MERCER has been a regular soldier and a BBC correspondent, and has written three novels. He is now the MP for Newark.

A Poem Turned into a Sword

CHARLES ELLIOTT

Possibly because we wish we were creative, but aren't, publishing editors like me tend to be proprietary about the books we publish. You'll frequently hear an editor speak of 'my' book, meaning not that he or she has written it, or seriously edited it, or in fact done much more than read it. Still, it's 'my' book.

I've always regarded this as a fairly innocent practice. It doesn't hurt anyone and it makes the editor feel better, something that – given his hours and rate of pay – he roundly deserves. And it contributes a powerful incentive to the publishing operation itself. A book is often successful exactly to the degree that everybody involved in publishing it is personally enthusiastic about it, and this enthusiasm generally starts with a possessive editor.

The Woman Warrior was my book. I say this not to avoid accusations of *parti pris* – after all, everybody who writes about a book for *Slightly Foxed* can by definition be accused of that – but simply to make clear where I come from. In the winter of 1975 an agent sent the manuscript to Alfred A. Knopf, Inc. in New York, where I was a senior editor. It ended up in my hands, because I was supposed to be the house China expert. (I had picked up some Mandarin when I was in the army.) I remember reading it in a bleak, smoke-filled room in the Criminal Court Building on Centre Street while waiting for jury duty, and being stunned. I had never read anything like it

---

Maxine Hong Kingston, *The Woman Warrior: Memoirs of a Girlhood among Ghosts* (1976)
Picador · Pb · 176pp · £8.99 · ISBN 9780330264006

before. I convinced my boss to take it on for publication.

Maxine Ting Ting Hong Kingston, I learned, was a young Chinese-American woman; this was her first book, in fact her first publication of any kind, apart from a story for which she received a prize when she was (I think) 8 years old. Yet there was in the clarity and control she displayed, as well as her narrative precision, real mastery. Beyond that, far beyond that, there was the terrible richness of the stories she had to tell. If there was one thing the book accomplished, it was to explode for good and all the Western assumption that Chinese literature was no more than a heap of chinoiserie.

Maxine grew up in Stockton, a fairly poor agricultural town north-east of San Francisco. Her parents were minimally integrated immigrants from South China. The atmosphere in the Hong home was still intensely Chinese, peasant Chinese; to the family, the white world outside was in many ways a mysterious place 'full of machines and ghosts – Taxi Ghosts, Bus Ghosts, Police Ghosts, Fire Ghosts, Meter Reader Ghosts, Tree Trimming Ghosts, Five-and-Dime Ghosts'. Yet to Maxine the China of her mother and father was equally strange, especially as it emerges from the tales her mother tells her, the 'talk-story' that fires her imagination and shapes this book. So many of the stories are about women – about women and violence and bravery.

'No Name Woman', for example, describes an aunt who became pregnant long after her husband, along with so many of the other young men of the village, had sailed off to America. 'The village had also been counting,' her mother said.

> On the night the baby was to be born the villagers raided our house . . . At first they threw mud and rocks at the house. Then they threw eggs and started slaughtering our stock. We could hear the animals scream their deaths – the roosters, the pigs, the last great roar from the ox.

They smashed the house and ruined all the aunt's belongings. 'Your aunt gave birth in the pigsty that night. The next morning when I went for the water, I found her and the baby plugging up the family well.'

The aunt's name was never mentioned again, could never be mentioned again. It was as if she had never existed. Yet Maxine cannot resist speculating about her and the terrors that must have marked her life as a woman in a culture where women had few rights, and inhibitions were absolute. 'Adultery is an extravagance.' What could it have been like to commit it?

'Whenever she had to warn us about life, my mother told us stories that ran like this one.' But talk-story was not all warnings. It could also inspire. Maxine's mother – her name, appropriately, is Brave Orchid – makes plain that a girl did not need to grow up as a slave or a wife. She could be a heroine, a woman warrior like the legendary Fa Mu Lan. She could bring vengeance.

It is difficult to do justice to the chapter called 'White Tigers', in which Kingston imagines the education and training of a woman warrior. It is a brilliant amalgam of the hallucinatory and the absolutely specific, based upon legend but grounded in human detail, seamlessly moving back and forth between myth and the quotidian. She is trained in dragon ways; she learns 'to make my mind large, so that there is room for paradoxes'; she submits to having the list of grievances she is to avenge carved on her back with knives ('If an enemy should flay me, the light would shine through my skin like lace'). She assembles an army, acquires a husband and fights many battles, finally beheading the corrupt emperor and seating a peasant on the throne. In the end, having killed the fat greedy baron who has oppressed her family (he ineffectively pleads that people are happy to get rid of girl-children, 'maggots in the rice'), she returns to her home village and settles down. As her mother tells it, the tale is one of triumphant feminist power.

But not for the young Maxine. Her reality is far more complicated and painful. 'My American life has been such a disappointment.' Nobody cared about her straight As. 'You can't eat straight As.' And when one of her parents or a fellow emigrant villager remarked 'Feeding girls is feeding cowbirds', she would scream so hard that she couldn't stop. '"I'm not a bad girl," I would scream. "I'm not a bad girl. I'm not a bad girl." I might as well have said, "I'm not a girl."' And how could she save her village when she was not even sure what her village was?

Apart from Maxine herself, the most extraordinary character in *The Woman Warrior* is her mother Brave Orchid. In China, before she emigrated to join her husband, Brave Orchid took the unusual and daring step of enrolling in a college of midwifery in Canton, and spent two years learning to be a doctor. The students there were China's 'new women, scientists who changed the rituals'. So when Brave Orchid returned with her degree to New Society Village, she was welcomed as someone with knowledge of a wonderful and unfamiliar kind. She set broken bones and brought babies into the world safely and acted as 'a capable exorcist'. After all, there were still ghosts to be dealt with. Yet as if no revolution had ever occurred in this 'new' China, she had a slave girl, purchased at the Canton market with care and hard bargaining. America was for her a terrible comedown – no more doctoring, but hard work in her husband's laundry and, after urban renewal brought that enterprise to an end, stoop labour in the tomato fields. Nothing, however, diminished her energy or constrained her splendid passion for talk-story.

At the very end of the book Maxine Kingston offers an apposite bit of talk-story of her own, the true tale of the poetess Ts'ai Yen, who in the second century AD was captured by a barbarian prince and bore him two children. She spent twelve years away from China before being ransomed, twelve years of alienation and homesickness. But she brought back a poem called 'Eighteen Stanzas for a Barbarian Reed Pipe' that somehow bridges the distance between the cultures and is still sung by Chinese. 'It translated well.'

Knopf published *The Woman Warrior* in September 1976 in a small printing. Needless to say, I talked it up. For a while it received only modest, though enthusiastic, attention from reviewers, until John Leonard, the chief daily book critic of the *New York Times*, weighed in with what can only be called the ultimate selling review. 'A remarkable book has just been published,' he wrote. 'It is one of the best I've read in years . . . It burns the fat right out of the mind. As a dream – of the female avenger – it is dizzying, elemental, a poem turned into a sword.' What can I say, except that Leonard was right?

In the years since, plenty of people have agreed with him. Garlanded with prizes, *The Woman Warrior* now exists in dozens of translations (including Chinese) and has sold – in America alone – well over 1.5 million copies. Not *Fifty Shades of Grey*, perhaps, but quite enough to please any proprietary editor puffing 'his' book.

CHARLES ELLIOTT is a retired editor and author of several books of essays, the latest of which is *Why Every Man Needs a Tractor.*

Championing the Underdog

JUSTIN MAROZZI

From Herodotus' and Thucydides' time the war book has been with us as an ever-present literary companion to the massacres on the battlefield. I took Norman Lewis's *Naples '44* to Iraq with me in 2004 and found its humanity and honesty instantly compelling. Graham Greene considered Lewis 'one of our best writers, not of any particular decade but of our century', and during the darker days in Iraq it was strangely comforting to realize that there is little new in conflict. From 'friendly fire' and war profiteers to prostitution and petty bureaucracy, it has all been seen before.

Much of war is tragedy and farce, and Lewis has the reporter's eye to observe it in telling detail with prose that is by turns laconic, angry and arresting. *Naples '44* finds him appointed an intelligence officer in the Field Security Service, having escaped 'the drudgery of delivering army-style, pay-attention-you-fuckers lectures' and joined the invasion convoy bound for Salerno, attached to the headquarters staff of the American Fifth Army. General Clark, 'the destroying angel of Southern Italy', has reduced much of the region to scorched despair, though the smaller towns have escaped bombing: 'The only visible damage to most villages had been the inevitable sack of the post office by the vanguard of the advancing troops, who seem to have been philatelists to a man.'

Bureaucracy is one of the lead villains in these pages. The mystified Lewis marvels at the ever-expanding 'Black Book' of suspects,

Norman Lewis, *Naples '44* (1978)
Eland · Pb · 192pp · £10.99 · ISBN 9780907871729

teeming with same-surname families – 'Espositos and Gennaros turn up by the hundred' – and 'poetic idiocies' galore. Like all good intelligence officers, he gets dirt under his fingernails and forges relationships with an extraordinary cast of characters. These include comic cameos like Professor Placella who has a profitable and unusual line in surgery. 'He boasts that his replacement hymen is much better than the original, and that – costing only 10,000 lire – it takes the most vigorous husband up to three nights to demolish it.'

Lewis inspires confessions in friends, colleagues and acquaintances. As the confidant of an anxious British officer and his voracious Neapolitan lover he does his best to help with affairs of the heart – and of the bed.

> She had made him understand by gestures one could only shudderingly imagine that her late husband – although half-starved, and even when in the early stages of tuberculosis from which he died – never failed to have intercourse with her less than six times a night. She also had a habit, which terrified Frazer, of keeping an eye on the bedside clock while he performed. I recommended him to drink – as the locals did – marsala with the yolks of eggs stirred into it, and to wear a medal of San Rocco, patron of coitus reservatus, which could be had in any religious-supplies shop.

More often than not, sex does not equate to romance in Lewis's wartime Naples. Extreme poverty and near-starvation have reduced many women to prostitution. War corrupts everyone it touches. Among the many cinematic set-pieces is the ghastly scene in a vast municipal building where working-class housewives have gathered to offer their bodies in return for tins of army food.

> The women kept absolutely still, they said nothing, and their faces were as empty of expression as graven images. They might have been selling fish, except that this place lacked the excitement of a fish market. There was no soliciting, no suggestion,

no enticement, not even the discreetest and most accidental display of flesh. The boldest of the soldiers had pushed themselves, tins in hand, to the front, but now, faced with these matter-of-fact family-providers driven here by empty larders, they seemed to flag. Once again reality had betrayed the dream and the air fell limp.

Lewis's Naples is an inferno of suffering. Unthinkable shortages of food and water carry off the weak, the young and the elderly. Families have lost their clothes and possessions in the indiscriminate bombings. Strange apparitions stalk the streets dressed in whatever comes to hand, 'a man in an old dinner-jacket, knickerbockers and army boots', women in dresses made from curtains. The Neapolitan aristocracy has been reduced to draughty, high-ceilinged apartments in their once grand palazzos. At best, furniture is a rickety table, a chair and a bed. Food is almost non-existent. Lewis gets to know Vincente Lattarullo, a penniless, unemployed lawyer who becomes a stalwart friend. He can only afford to eat once a day, 'a little bread dipped in olive oil, into which was rubbed a tomato'. Even to pay for this he must double up as a *Zio di Roma*, acting as 'an uncle from Rome' to add patrician glamour to provincial funerals.

Mary Kuper

With their lives disintegrating, Neapolitans take refuge in superstition. They queue to implore the help of saints and worry that the blood of San Gennaro, patron saint of Naples, may not liquefy as it does every year. 'Naples has reached a state of nervous exhaustion when mass hallucination has become a commonplace, and belief of any kind can be more real than reality.'

War brings out the worst in many of those in Lewis's forensic field of view. Denunciations are a daily, diary-filling event. Many, perhaps most, are false and entirely malevolent. Official cruelty lurks everywhere. Lewis hears the scarcely credible news that American soldiers of the 45th Division have been ordered 'not only to take no German prisoners, but to use the butts of their rifles to beat to death those who try to surrender'. Officers mull half-baked plans to send syphilitic prostitutes to infect customers in the German-occupied north. The pettiness, small-mindedness, inhumanity and corruption of the occupation are recurring themes.

Lewis has a gimlet-eyed appreciation of the futility of his work. Appointed as head of security for a number of small towns within the orbit of Naples, he notes that all fall within the territory of the deadly Camorra. 'The task is a hopeless one, and it would be demoralising to take it too seriously,' not least because military officers at the very highest level are in partnership with the Camorra and the black-market racket.

Suffering falls on young and old alike. Empty-stomached boys jumping into the back of supply lorries to raid rations have their fingers hacked off by American bayonets. On 1 November 1943, contemplating a menu offering either disguised dogfish or horsemeat, Lewis watches a group of blind orphan girls enter the restaurant scavenging for food. Each child is sobbing.

The experience changed my outlook. Until now I had clung to the comforting belief that human beings eventually come to terms with pain and sorrow. Now I understood I was wrong, and like Paul I suffered a conversion – but to pessimism. These little girls, any one of whom could be my daughter, came into the restaurant weeping, and they were weeping when they were led away. I knew that, condemned to everlasting darkness, hunger and loss, they would weep on incessantly. They would never recover from their pain and I would never recover from the memory of it.

Yet this nascent pessimism cannot undermine Lewis's innate humanity. He is forever going the extra mile – sometimes literally – to help the beleaguered civilian population around him, bending rules to prevent the horrifyingly casual imposition of martial law death penalties, smuggling food to friends and always struggling against the miscarriage of justice.

In *Naples '44* we see the horrors of war, together with its dangerous allure and unmatched intensity. Perhaps it was this experience that helped propel Lewis into a lifetime of far-flung reporting from dangerous parts and an admirable career championing the underdog. In 1968, his coruscating *Sunday Times* article 'Genocide' exposed the Brazilian government's criminal treatment of the country's indigenous tribes – mass murder, torture, sexual abuse, land theft – and led, a year later, to the foundation of Survival International, the movement for tribal peoples.

The roots of this outrage at man's inhumanity can surely be traced back to Lewis's time in Naples, a 'perfumed Arcadia' reduced by war to a Dantean hell.

JUSTIN MAROZZI is writing a history of Baghdad, where he has spent much of the past seven years (www.justinmarozzi.com). He is still hoping to turn his hand to war satire one of these days.

A Bath with a View

CAROLINE CHAPMAN

I once met Sybille Bedford. 'Met' is perhaps the wrong word; I pounced on her at a crowded Time-Life party and began raving about her novel *A Legacy* which I had just read. She looked at me vaguely. 'Another lunatic', I could see her thinking. Then we were separated in the crush, much to her relief I suspect. Sybille, I feel sure, was not one to suffer fools gladly.

On the back cover of her memoir *Quicksands*, published a year before her death in 2006, is a remarkable photograph. It shows Sybille sitting naked in a large marble bath, reading from a sheaf of A4 pages. It is a startling image, and it provides clues to several aspects of her life and singular personality.

Sybille in her eyrie
© Evelyn Gendel

The photograph was taken in 1950 by Evelyn Gendel, Sybille's close companion for several years – an attachment she described as one of her happiest. The bath plus an L-shaped studio and small kitchen were contained within 'a longish kind of shed' perched on the roof of an office block in the Piazza di Spagna in Rome. To reach her eyrie she had to climb up five floors and a flight of wooden steps. For Sybille, the inconvenience of this ascent counted for nothing when compared

Sybille Bedford, *A Legacy* (1956) · Penguin · Pb · 384pp · £10.99 · ISBN 9780141188058; *Quicksands: A Memoir* (2005) · Penguin · Pb · 384pp · £8.99 · ISBN 9780140279764.

with the incomparable view it gave her over the rooftops of Rome. The shed came to her, as did so many things in her life, through the kindness of friends; in this instance Theodora and Constantine FitzGibbon, who were leaving Rome and wanted someone to take on the unfinished lease of their 'flat'.

The sheaf of papers could well be a section of *A Legacy*, since it was during these contented years with Evelyn that she wrote the novel. On close examination the pages appear to be covered with her famously atrocious handwriting: although Sybille had taught herself to read, her formal education was so brief and fragmentary that she had never been taught how to write. The eyeshade was a necessity as she suffered from an intolerance of glare – a particular hazard for someone who spent much of her life living within sight of the Mediterranean.

She craved the warm south intensely, and used it as the setting for her other three published novels – so it comes as a surprise to find that much of the action of *A Legacy* takes place in pre-First World War Germany, principally in Berlin. But she herself was born there, in 1911, the daughter of Baron Maximilian von Schoenebeck and Elizabeth Bernard, his German-Jewish wife, both of whom share some of the circumstances and characteristics of their fictitious counterparts.

A Legacy is written from the point of view of a young child (Francesca/Sybille) brought up among adults who looks back to the time before she was born. 'Thus what I know or feel I know', she wrote, 'about the places and the men and women in this story is derived from what I saw and above all heard and overheard as a child at the age of roughly three to ten, much of which I managed to absorb, retain and, decades after, to re-shape in an adult mode.'

In other words, the book is largely autobiographical, as are all but one of her novels. If you read them all on the trot, as I have just done, the line between fact and fiction becomes hopelessly blurred. But Sybille's life was so extraordinary that one can understand her obsessive attempts to make some sense of it. 'Is everything only what we remember it to be – neither more nor less? Where, then, and when is truth?'

The plot of *A Legacy* revolves around the lives of three families and the way they react to a set of circumstances. Grandmama and Grandpapa Merz and their grown-up progeny occupy an 'outrageously large and ugly' house in a fashionable area of Berlin. They are Jewish, wealthy, sedentary, and isolated by choice from society. The house is run by the butler, the omnipresent Gottlieb, the only one apparently capable of making a decision. Amid the suffocating gloom of the décor, the family frequently assembles to eat gargantuan meals and discuss the goings-on of its members. Their eldest son, Edu, is a weak-willed gambler entirely dominated by his wife Sarah, one of the book's most compelling characters.

The second family occupies a very different sphere: Catholic landed gentry living in their ancestral *schloss* in a rural corner of Baden. Motherless from an early age, Julius (the book's main character, 'at once delicate and worldly, and much affected by lapses that were neither') and his three brothers are brought up by their eccentric father Baron Felden to be cultured country gentlemen.

The Merzes and the Feldens are united by the marriage of Julius to the Merzes' docile daughter Melanie, who dies of TB soon after giving birth to a daughter (Sybille's actual half-sister). When Julius remarries, this time to Caroline, a beautiful Englishwoman, the Merzes continue to treat him – and, by extension, Caroline – as one of the family. A daughter is born to Julius and Caroline – who is Sybille in all but name.

What precipitates the book's inciting incident is the unification of Germany in 1870. 'No good would come of it, said the old Baron, and his tenants said the same.' But the tenor of the times requires that his sons should take up careers: Julius as a diplomat, his younger brother Johannes as a soldier. Johannes is duly sent to a Prussian military cadet school at Benzheim. Appalled by its brutality and inhumanity, he escapes and returns home more dead than alive. The school demands his immediate return. The old Baron refuses to comply.

'Then several kinds of forces began to move all at once. They were not directly interested in Johannes, he was discounted and at the same time [became] a factor in their calculations, and they crushed him.' These conflicting 'forces' consisted of the German War Office and the authorities at Benzheim, the Feldens and, last but certainly not least, Count Bernin, father of Clara who is engaged to Julius's eldest brother Gustavus. Bernin, the leader of a powerful Catholic clique, is wealthy, influential and ambitious.

The newspapers take up the story and Johannes becomes the centre of a *cause célèbre*. There is a good deal of arm-twisting all round. Bernin, for one, is told he will be 'rendering a lasting service to the German Government' if he facilitates Johannes's return to Benzheim. He resists. But Benzheim wins in the end and Johannes, now no longer wholly sane, is sent back. There is a desperate bid to save the boy which ends in a tragic accident; and a vital letter is not delivered which, in time, leads to yet another tragedy. Few of those involved feel entirely blameless for what has happened.

When I first read *A Legacy* I assumed the title referred to the ripples that spread outwards from this sequence of events. But in her 1999 introduction to the novel, Sybille explained her choice thus:

> Much of what was allowed to happen in these decades [1870–1914] was ill-conceived, cruel, bad (in simple terms); there was also a German dottiness, devoid of humour . . . Is some of this a foundation of the vast and monstrous thing that followed? Did the private events I lightly draw upon leave some legacy? Writing about them made me think so. Hence the title.

She once said that she had written *A Legacy* out of a loathing for Germany and, apart from one brief visit with Aldous Huxley in 1932, she did not return there until the 1960s. She also made a conscious decision to abandon her native tongue and write in English. At heart she was a European – little wonder since she lived in Germany with her father until his death when she was 14, and her adolescence was spent partly with her mother in Italy and France, partly on her own in England. She was to continue this peripatetic and often precarious pattern throughout her life.

This is reflected in her writing: the text of *A Legacy* is peppered with French and German sentences, even entire paragraphs. If your idiomatic French is a bit rusty, tough. 'No one', she once said, 'has ever done anything worth doing who thought about the reader', and this attitude is – for me – one of the great attractions of her books: she constantly challenges you to keep up with her. If you fail for instance to realize that three of the characters having lunch on the terrace are monkeys – too bad. (I retained a clear image of this lunch party from my original reading and wondered if I had carelessly missed an earlier clue. But I checked, and there was nothing to indicate their identity for five pages, although three of the guests did appear to be behaving rather oddly.)

Sybille is brilliant at evoking time and place: the cicada-loud, pine-scented heat of the French Riviera; the claustrophobic opulence of the Merzes' house in Berlin; the barbarism of the cadet school; the wit and sparkle of conversation among women of intellect and culture (she is particularly good at strong women); the mouth-watering food. And her dialogue is superb: in three words she can convey volumes.

A Legacy leaves you dazzled by its artistry, originality and sureness of touch. Deftly, she ties all the ends together – with one exception. Following a series of hilarious events involving Julius and his monkeys, he is obliged to donate two of them to the zoo – but what happened to the third?

CAROLINE CHAPMAN has recently published a biography of the founders of the Bowes Museum in County Durham and is now researching a character who played a pivotal role in the Grand Tour.

Feverish Haste

BENJAMIN WHITROW

In 2005 an excellent article by Lucy Lethbridge about Denton Welch appeared in *Slightly Foxed*. So why another? Well, he is one of those writers who attract a small but passionate band of devotees. Though regarded as a minor author by many, much as Saki is, or Nancy Mitford or Henry Green, he has nothing in common with any of these. He is unique, and my love of his books has continued throughout my reading life.

Welch was born in 1915 and died in 1948. Almost everything he wrote is in the first person and based on real events in his life. He describes things exactly as they happened with a disciplined and assured spontaneity. As Edith Sitwell commented, 'He is a born writer. He never fumbles.' I discovered his writing when I was very young, at a time when I identified completely with his adolescent self. He was still alive then, and I wish now that I had thought to write to him. I first found his story 'The Judas Tree' at a time when copies of *Penguin New Writing* could be picked up for 6d. In it Welch relates how, as an art student, he was accosted by an obsessed, slightly crazed ex-school-

Mark Handley

Denton Welch, *Maiden Voyage* (1943) · Faber Finds · Pb · 258pp · £12 · ISBN 9780571280230; *In Youth Is Pleasure* (1944) · Enitharmon Press · Hb · 264pp · £15 · ISBN 9781904634171; *A Voice through a Cloud* (1950) · Enitharmon Press · Hb · 230pp · £15 · ISBN 9781904634065; *Journals* (2011) · Faber Finds · Pb · 392pp · £15 · ISBN 9780571282630; *Where Nothing Sleeps: The Complete Short Stories and Other Related Works* (2005) · Tartarus · Hb · 788pp · 2 vols. in slipcase · £70 · ISBN 9781872621944.

master who lured him back to his house in Greenwich and beseeched him to paint Judas Iscariot, hanging from a tree with his tongue black and lolling. He must have red hair, he insisted. We feel the young man's discomfort at finding himself so trapped. As the school-master leans over him, he can smell 'the juicy pipe tobacco, the animal smell of tweeds, and something between alcohol and the smell in chemist shops'. We know this man. Welch engages all the senses, touch and smell especially, to describe things and people. Now when I reread this story, I identify more strongly with the sad, pathetic old man desperately attempting to hold back time and sat-isfy his yearnings before it is too late.

I searched for more of Welch's books and will always remember the excitement when I found his selected journals in a blue Boots Library copy, thumbed and stained, with a metal hole at the base of the spine. I didn't know he had written a journal. Later I came across a Readers' Union copy of his unfinished autobiographical novel *A Voice through a Cloud* (1950). Inside was a handout with a photograph of an aesthetic but conventionally dressed young man staring soul-fully through thick 1940s spectacles. And in an article by Maurice Cranston I learned of the accident that had fractured his spine when in 1935 he was knocked off his bicycle by a car. He was 20. Cranston wrote that from that moment Welch became 'at once a boy and an old, old man', combining the intense, raw passion of youth and a feverish haste that stemmed from not knowing how much time he had left.

Once I had found all his published books – his fictionalized auto-biography of his early years in China, *Maiden Voyage* (1943), his novel *In Youth Is Pleasure* (1944) and the posthumously published collec-tions of short stories, *Brave and Cruel* (1949) and *A Last Sheaf* (1951) – I began to meet other people who liked his work. A postman who lived in Kent spent all his spare time visiting the churches and houses Welch wrote of in his diaries. Anne Rothenstein had inherited from her uncle, the art historian John Rothenstein, a cactus apparently potted up by Denton, now huge and adorning her piano. I was allowed to touch it.

In the early 1970s I searched out more people who had known him. One of these was Noël Adeney, a painter who had lent Welch the house in Kent where he lived his last few years. She had written a book called *No Coward Soul*, based on the letters he had written her and very hard to find now. She in turn had known Eric Oliver, the man with whom Welch fell in love and who looked after him so devotedly. I began to discover that, as often happens when a writer dies, vicious feuds ensued. Noël would not speak of Eric; she claimed she did not know where he lived. Her book describes the rivalry between them. My conclusion was that she also was in love with Denton.

In due course I did meet Eric. I had been reading some of Welch's stories on the radio and he wrote to thank me. I had always imagined that he was 'a bit of rough', but he was charming and cultured, very shy and strangely reluctant to say much about Welch. I knew that he had disposed of many of the manuscripts, which are now housed at the University of Texas. All he had left were Welch's ashes, which he kept on top of his wardrobe. However, he did tell me that a type-script of the complete journals was in the hands of one of Welch's friends, who would not let it go. This was the working copy Jocelyn Brooke had used when he edited them for publication in 1952.

In 1976 I eventually met this friend. His name was Francis Streeten. In a letter written before our meeting he told me 'he had the invidious distinction of appearing in several of Denton's stories'. He came to London to see a play I was in. I had no difficulty afterwards in spotting him – a large, almost elephantine man with a brown complexion, decorously picking his way towards the stage door. Welch's descriptions were often cruel, but they were also accurate.

We went to Fortnum's for tea. As we talked I noticed with delight all the strange characteristics that Welch had noted in Francis thirty years earlier – the baby voice, the tittering laugh 'as if someone was tickling his feet with a feather', the nicotine-stained fingers 'like chipolatas'. I liked his literate and articulate mind and his 1930s manner. He said he had been surprised by Denton's fame. Of all the friends they mixed with, he believed him to be the least interesting. Of course, I thought. They said that of Jane Austen and of Thomas Hardy. It's the one who sits at the back taking it all in who produces the work of genius.

The next year Francis died. His niece asked if I would go to the funeral with her and afterwards to his flat in St Leonards to help her rescue some family things. It was a sad day, with only a token few present at the service. The flat was on the top floor of an Edwardian block. That hot August afternoon we had to compete with the fleas as we picked our way over the unwashed dishes and discarded shirts. The sofa was piled high with detective novels. The wardrobe, full of new shirts still in their wrappings, had a bottom drawer that had been pulled on to the floor close to the unmade bed. In it was a cardboard box covered with cobwebs. Had Francis left it purposely on view? Without looking we knew it contained the journals.

After some negotiation with the family, I was allowed to take them away, promising to try to get them published. The typescript was scored and pasted together where Jocelyn Brooke had made his selections, and some of it was hard to decipher. I couldn't risk ripping it apart, so had to hold the pages up to the light to read what was typed underneath. It was a slow but exciting business. For almost a year I spent my spare time typing it out in duplicate. Then, by a lucky coincidence, I learned that Allison & Busby were planning to reissue the selected journals, and that a biography was to be written.

So it was that I was able to pass on the complete journals, which were edited by Michael De-la-Noy and published for the first time in this country in 1984. His biography *Denton Welch: The Making of a Writer* came out in the same year. There was also an exhibition of Welch's paintings at Abbott and Holder's gallery in Bloomsbury. The writer I loved was suddenly being talked about by the literati. I had mixed feelings about this. I was pleased he was getting the recognition he deserved, but I wondered how long it would last.

Ten years ago a further biography appeared. The author, James Methuen-Campbell, had managed to meet many people who had known Welch and track down many of his paintings, which were beautifully reproduced in the book. He also persuaded the same publisher, Tartarus, to bring out in two huge volumes all the known stories.

Denton Welch began to write because he had read and enjoyed J. R. Ackerley's *Hindoo Holiday*. He thought he would try to write a similar diary about how he ran away from school. He quickly discovered that he had almost perfect recall. The solitude enforced by his accident concentrated his memory, as it does sometimes with ill or elderly people who remember vividly and afresh things that have not been thought of for years. And he wrote it down just as it had occurred, in simple and disciplined prose.

Many people have speculated as to what Welch would have made of his life had he lived longer. I believe he would have gained recognition as a painter, but the pleasure of enjoying the active life that was denied him would not have induced him to write anything of significance. He himself admitted that he found a serenity in writing that he had never known before. It is our gain that he did.

BENJAMIN WHITROW is an actor who, during a long career, has worked for both the National Theatre and the RSC. He is perhaps best known for his role as Mr Bennet in the BBC production of *Pride and Prejudice*, but he is also proud to have been a reviewer for Alan Ross's *London Magazine*.

An Eye for Absurdity

ANTHONY GARDNER

Village fêtes are dangerous places to buy books. The conviction that somewhere among the ancient almanacs and dog-eared Jilly Coopers lurks an underpriced treasure is so strong that I find it hard to come away empty-handed, and habitually end up with a selection of curios I will never read. But now and again I strike lucky, as I did with my 1966 first edition of Michael Frayn's *The Russian Interpreter*.

Two things attracted me to it: I had read and loved another of Frayn's early novels, *Towards the End of the Morning*, and my girl-friend (now wife) was a translator from Russian. The book didn't leave me much the wiser about the language, but it did afford me a great deal of laughter – a rare achievement for a novel set in Moscow at the height of the Cold War.

I had interviewed Frayn a year before and noticed that a poster for *Wild Honey* (his translation of an early play by Chekhov) had pride of place in his hallway. I knew that he had been taught Russian while doing national service, but only learned much later that he had been a frequent visitor to the USSR in the Fifties and Sixties – which explains why his portrait of a maddening city where everything is 'unnecessarily complicated, never more than half explained' is so convincing.

The book's protagonist, Paul Manning, is a Cambridge graduate completing his studies in Administrative Management Sciences at Moscow University. Weighed down by the glumness of his sur-

Michael Frayn, *The Russian Interpreter* (1966)
Faber · Pb · 192pp · £6.99 · ISBN 9780571225057

roundings, he finds life made suddenly more interesting by the arrival of a mysterious compatriot. Frayn's opening paragraph brilliantly sets the tone for the novel, its words dancing an elegant, convoluted quadrille which foreshadows the spirals of the plot:

> Manning's old friend Proctor-Gould was in Moscow, and anxious to get in touch with him. Or so Manning was informed. He looked forward to the meeting. He had few friends in Moscow, none of them old friends, and no friends at all, old or new, in Moscow or anywhere else, called Proctor-Gould.

When the two finally meet, Proctor-Gould proves far from the smooth operator Paul has come to expect. Moon-faced and seedy in appearance, his drink of choice is not a vodka Martini but Nescafé; his chief characteristic is a nervous tugging of his ear lobe. As for his business, its exact nature is the question mark at the centre of the book: does he really, as he claims, recruit ordinary Russians to give their views to the Western media? Paul immediately wonders whether he is a spy – but cannot conceive of a less likely one.

Persuaded to act as Proctor-Gould's interpreter, Paul joins him on a round of official functions; but when he is asked to assist in his private affairs, the job becomes more challenging. On a country excursion Paul falls for the beautiful Raya, only to see her transfer her affections to Proctor-Gould and install herself in his hotel room. Since Raya speaks no English, Paul has to act as their go-between; and when Raya starts stealing Proctor-Gould's possessions, the situation becomes more complicated still.

Given Frayn's later success with *Noises Off*, it isn't surprising that *The Russian Interpreter* has a strong element of farce. Raya's thefts become a wonderful running gag – no sooner has one object been recovered than another disappears – which is all the funnier because she makes no attempt to conceal or excuse them. When Proctor-Gould tries to protect some precious books by locking them in his luggage, Raya solves the problem by walking off with an entire suitcase.

The whole premise of the novel is, of course, rich in comic possibilities. On the one hand there is the inability of two people to make any sense of each other; on the other, the interpreter's freedom to take liberties with the messages he is asked to convey.

> 'Gordon is a good judge of women,' she said. 'He knows how to appreciate them, and how to deal with them. Tell him so.'
>
> 'She says you know how to suck up to people,' Manning told Proctor-Gould sourly.

In the book's most hilarious scene, Paul drinks too much at a tedious faculty dinner and reduces Proctor-Gould's fulsome speech to two sentences – only to find to his horror that he has delivered them in English rather than Russian. Frayn also treats us to some brilliant similes ('He threw the words away casually, almost surreptitiously, as if they were old sweet wrappers he was disposing of in the street') and excellent deadpan jokes:

> From the loudspeakers among the trees came the slow movement of a violin concerto, austere and heartbreaking. On such a morning people walked gravely with a sense that the world was well-ordered and poignant.
>
> 'That music, Paul,' sighed Proctor-Gould. 'The whole soul of Russia is in it.'
>
> 'It's Bach,' said Manning shortly.

But the novel also has a darker side. Like Kafka, Frayn understands that the dividing line between farce and horror is a thin one, and when Paul is arrested he struggles – despite his innocence – to find a version of his strange story that will not incriminate him. In a country where the rights of the individual count for nothing, his requests to speak to the British Embassy or be told what charges he faces begin to sound ridiculous even to himself.

Frayn has serious points, too, to make about the use of language. Proctor-Gould may be helpless in his private conversations with Raya, but he is able to make headway with the Soviet authorities because he uses the same abstract, impersonal phrases they do ('the cultural treasure house we share', 'setting our barren suspicions and fears behind us'). The Russian characters, meanwhile, struggle in a world of communist jargon: Paul's dissident friend Katerina is chillingly hampered by 'a record of negative contribution'.

Katerina is the book's most engaging character, and her presence is a homage to the Russian tradition of philosophical novels: between his adventures with Proctor-Gould, Paul roams the streets with her discussing the nature of the universe. But whereas Dostoevsky's characters are happy to go on musing for page after page, Katerina has the gift of encapsulating her thoughts in a few memorable sentences. When Paul tells her that he cannot understand her perception of God, she replies, 'Nor do I. We couldn't expect to. All we can do is venture descriptions of Him which give rise to unfathomable infinities and unresolvable contradictions, and to contemplate these with humility.'

For me, one of the fascinating things about the novel is the way it prefigures a play Frayn was to write thirty years later. In *Copenhagen*'s most striking scene, a walk taken by the physicist Heisenberg is compared with the movement of an electron through a cloud chamber. In *The Russian Interpreter* Paul imagines 'himself, Katya, and the people crowding off trolley-buses . . . as nothing but a complexly interbalanced network of electrical charges'. Later he reflects on the strangeness of human beings: 'How odd and unfamiliar were the relations between them, like the interactions of half-understood particles beneath the microscope.'

The Russian Interpreter also curiously anticipates today's reality TV culture. 'The Press and television', Proctor-Gould tells Paul, 'want to get away from the professionals. They want to get at the real flesh-and-blood people who make up the other 99.9% of the world.' He adds that '*everyone* has . . . a personality the public would be interested to explore' (an idea that Andy Warhol would define two years later as 'famous for fifteen minutes'). Paul's head of department responds incisively and refreshingly: 'I must tell you frankly, being a personality in your sense seems to me a little like being a prostitute.'

If *The Russian Interpreter* is impressively prophetic, it is also a valuable time capsule. The system that seemed immovable forty-five years ago has gone, and the cityscape of Moscow is changing; but should future generations wish to picture the capital of communism in its heyday, they will find few better descriptions than this:

He crossed the great empty plaza in front of the university, watched impassively by the gigantic gimcrack statues thirty floors above of women grasping hammers and cog-wheels. Everything seemed enormous and out-of-scale . . . Beyond the plaza, in a formal vista of ornamental gardens, solitary pedestrians moved like Bedouin, separated from one another by Saharas of empty brown flower-bed and drying tarmacadam. They were so small they seemed merely an infestation. The authorities should have put human-being powder down and got rid of them.

Frayn's recent memoir *My Father's Fortune* gives only tantalizing glimpses of the period of his life in which he wrote this novel. Rereading *The Russian Interpreter* made me hungry for a fuller autobiography, recounting his own adventures in the Soviet Union. With his brilliant eye for absurdity, it is the land he was born to write about.

ANTHONY GARDNER's Russian vocabulary is almost non-existent, but he is very pleased to have discovered the word троллейбус (pronounced 'trolley-bus'). It denotes a trolley-bus. He is the editor of the Royal Society of Literature *Review*, and the author of a novel, *The Rivers of Heaven*.

Rolling down to Rio

TREVOR FISHLOCK

Between the ages of 7 and 11 I often saw my father take the stage in a packed and smoky concert hall. It was a once-a-week performance. Sometimes I watched from the wings as he took command of the spotlight. Applause subsided into hush. The pianist rippled an intro and Father drew deep, hauling his baritone from his belly and delivering each word bright and clear.

He always started with a rollick and had the crowd by the lapels as he launched into one of his favourites: 'When the Sergeant-Major's on Parade'. Then he changed the pace to something lyrical before cantering through 'Old Father Thames'. As far as I remember he was never a microphone man and his thrilling 'Holy City' came close to rattling the beer glasses at the back. After another sweet number he fired on all cylinders with 'The Floral Dance' and exited in a storm of cheers.

This was in the late 1940s and early '50s. No one sings like that now; and there are no smoky concert halls.

Father's style was foursquare and manly, a chip off the old Edwardian balladeer. Slight portliness added gravitas. And he was jovial. He performed at regimental dinners and concerts, entertained patients in hospital and once sang to inmates at a prison. He also poured himself into Regency breeches and donned a powdered wig, but that was a spectacle before my time.

It was because everyone said he sounded like the great Peter Dawson that, more than thirty years ago, I bought a second-hand

---

Peter Dawson, *Fifty Years of Song* (1951), is out of print.

copy of Dawson's autobiography and some of the numerous recordings he made.

The book is called *Fifty Years of Song*; and, indeed, Dawson sang into his seventies. He bestrode the gramophone age, recording more than 3,000 songs and selling millions of copies. He landed in London from his native Adelaide in 1903. He was 21 and had little money but possessed a remarkable voice and a top hat and tails. In this rig he arrived at the door of the baritone Sir Charles Santley who became his teacher and mentor. From four years of classical study with Santley and others he emerged as a bass-baritone with a mastery of two octaves and of the oratorios *Elijah*, *Messiah* and *The Creation*.

Newly married and pressed to earn a living, Dawson entered the rough-and-tumble of London commercial music. His wife rounded up a few pennies for his bus fare to a studio where in 1904 he made his first recording, on a wax cylinder. He sang into a recording horn while an Edison Bell engineer disconcertingly pushed and pulled his shoulder, rocking him backward and forward for voice balance.

A tedious aspect of cylinder recording was that a master yielded few copies. Dawson had to make many masters, singing six hours a day over five days, lubricating his throat with lunchtime beer. But his pay of £75 bought a bed and wardrobe he and his wife badly needed. Later he became adept at controlling his voice balance, rocking in and out of the recording horn while a studio hand pranced around him clacking coconut shells for a horsey effect.

In a business ever-hungry for hits he and other singers resorted to piracy. They took miniature cylinder recorders into music halls to record new songs while shorthand writers scribbled the words. Magpies in human form, they were soon ready to record. It was an ingenious and shady use of new technology, and copyright legislation stopped it all. As a rising recording star, Dawson, for one, was grateful for his multiplying streams of royalties.

Like others, Dawson sang under pseudonyms to boost his earnings. When HMV asked him 'Can you sing Scottish?' he used the name of Hector Grant to sing the songs of the Scottish music-hall star Harry Lauder. Then he wrote a bunch of heathery songs and created a subsidiary career as a tartan balladeer. Disguised in kilt and wig Hector Grant played the Glasgow Coliseum for twelve weeks and no one knew he was Peter Dawson.

Dawson said that immaculate diction underpinned his success. 'Gramophone recording', he added, 'taught me more about correcting my enunciation than any teacher.'

Although a concert singer, highly regarded as a performer of Handel, Schubert, Wagner and Tchaikovsky, he did not commit himself to opera. 'It struck me', he said, 'as too much work for too little pay.' He got into trouble while appearing in *Die Meistersinger* at Covent Garden in 1909 for playing poker in the wings while waiting to perform. Scooping his winnings into a bag he went out to sing but dropped the bag. The coins rolled all over the stage.

His immense repertoire reflected the tastes of the age: 'The Bandolero', 'Yeomen of England', 'Boys of the Old Brigade', 'Drake's Drum', 'Rolling down to Rio', 'Waltzing Matilda', 'The Road to Mandalay', 'Glorious Devon', 'The Mountains of Mourne', 'Roses of Picardy', 'I Am a Friar of Orders Grey'.

In 1911 Katie Moss witnessed the traditional Furry Dance in Helston and boarded the train home full of excitement. Over the next hours she set down the scene in a song, 'The Floral Dance'. Peter Dawson recorded it the following year and, although some local grumps didn't like its reference to a 'quaint old Cornish town', he made the song a signature tune.

He himself was similarly inspired on a train journey. Reading Rudyard Kipling's marching poem 'Boots' on a train to Margate he found himself creating a tune for it. When he reached his hotel he demanded the use of a piano while the music still bubbled. He wrote it under his composer-alias of J. P. McCall and sang it at Sir Henry Wood's promenade concert in 1928. There was acclaim from everyone, except Sir Henry. 'Don't ever sing rubbish like that again,' he growled. 'Sing songs that uplift 'em. Brahms or Schubert.' Dawson stood his ground and Sir Henry recanted. 'Boots' became a Dawson special; and Kipling told him he liked it.

In the 1920s Dawson sang on 2LO, forerunner of the BBC, and he performed frequently for the BBC into the 1950s. He starred at the London Palladium. He also lent his name to advertising. He promoted cigarettes – 'No throat irritation' – and declared that 'Horlicks and I are old friends.' He made his last record in 1959 and died in Sydney in 1961 aged 79.

My father modelled his performances on Dawson's genial style and repertoire. When his military service ended he was a regimental sergeant-major casting around for a post-war job. Someone remembered his singing and organizational flair and he became manager of a south coast holiday camp, responsible for entertaining thousands who arrived with their ration books from the blitzed streets of London and the Midlands. They had shared the same experience, had been in uniform, and were looking for playtime in austerity.

Father rolled out the barrel and ran the sports days, the bathing-beauty show, the swimming races, the knobbly-knees and ugly-face contests, the fancy-dress show, the pub outing, tombola and tom-foolery. Radio and music-hall comedians and singers and magicians came to play. There was endless music and dancing, reveille and the camp song, and the vamp of a Naafi piano. In a way, the hokey-cokey was what it was all about. As the despot of fun, Father produced the highly popular home-made campers' concert, every act enthusiastically applauded, and he himself a star turn. But things changed, he started another career, the Dawson years ended, 'The Floral Dance' faded. Package holidays and rock 'n roll were on the way.

TREVOR FISHLOCK is a writer who was once an angelic choirboy.

Cape-bound

DERVLA MURPHY

Soon after my Dublin grandfather's death in 1946 several heavy tea-chests were delivered by rail to our Lismore home. My father gleefully pored over the numerous bulky tomes: the *Works* of Samuel Richardson in seven volumes (1785), a *History of Free Masonry* in five volumes, a rare numbered edition (No. 775) of the works of Henry Fielding in ten volumes with an introductory essay by Leslie Stephen, etc. etc. Being then aged 14 I was unexcited until I came upon a slim volume (foolscap octavo) by a mid-Victorian Englishwoman identifiable on p.1 as a kindred spirit. Ever since, Lucie Duff Gordon's *Letters from the Cape*, written to a devoted husband and a worried mother, has been among my favourite accounts of travel.

Lucie Austin had enjoyed an unconventional education, including a few terms at a Hampstead co-ed where she added Latin to her collection of languages. As an 18-year-old she translated Niebuhr's *Studies of Ancient Greek Mythology*, the first of many acclaimed translations. A year later she married Sir Alexander Duff Gordon, one of Queen Victoria's assistant gentleman ushers who was to become a senior civil servant. Until 1860 this happy couple's London home attracted literary lions (and a few lionesses) from near and far. Then Lucie developed an ominous cough and was advised to spend a year or so in the Cape Colony, a 'cure' often recommended to consumptives.

Characteristically, Lady Duff Gordon was averse to the new-fangled steamers ('you breathe coal-dust for the first ten days'). She

---

Lady Duff Gordon, *Letters from the Cape* (1864), is out of print, as is Katherine Frank's biography of Lucie, *A Passage to Egypt* (1994).

therefore embarked for Cape Town on a tall-masted ship and had a 'very enjoyable' two-month voyage despite an uncommon share of 'contrary winds and foul weather'. She shared a cabin with her maid Sally who neither grumbled nor gossiped and was always, like her mistress, amused and curious – 'a better companion than many more educated people'. The third member of the party was a white goat who yielded a pint of milk morning and evening – 'a great resource, as the tea and coffee are abominable'. This Maltese citizen at first disliked African grass but on the return journey, in May 1862, was still giving milk – until suddenly she died, 'to the general grief of the ship'.

When, towards the end of her journey, Sir Alexander proposed publishing his wife's letters, Lucie scoffed, 'You must have fallen into second childhood to think of *printing* such rambling hasty scrawls . . . I never could write a good letter . . .

Daniel Macklin

only I fancy *you* will be amused by some of my "impressions".' Her mother, Sarah Austin, eagerly supported Sir Alexander, noting Lucie's 'frank and high-toned originality'. In an introduction to the first (1864) edition she emphasized, as the strongest motive for publication, the value of her daughter's impressions as an antidote to the general tone of English travellers '[which] is too frequently arrogant and contemptuous' because they make no attempt 'to search out, under external differences, the proofs of a common nature'.

In contrast, this English traveller took individuals as she found them. The Cape's cultural cross-currents intrigued her. Near Newlands she observed a drainage scheme with an unexpected feature – 'the foreman a Caffre, black as ink, six feet three inches high, and broad in proportion, with a staid, dignified air, and Englishmen working under him!' In Wynberg an Irishwoman recalled shocking her puritanical Dutch host 'by admiring the naked Caffres who worked on his farm. He wanted them to wear clothes.' One would like to know more about this female admirer of naked males who sounds like a remnant of eighteenth-century Ireland.

Lucie provides many glimpses of everyday life in a singularly multiracial colony. Here were Hottentots, Dutch, Caffres, Germans, Malays, English, Malagasies, French, Mantatees, Irish, Bosjeman, Bastaards and boers, who had not yet graduated to capital letters. Most Cape Bastaards were the offspring, in various combinations, of white sailors, black slaves and Hottentots. By the 1860s, in a territory slightly larger than Britain, this mixum-gatherum was collaborating and interbreeding with minimal friction between the settlers and the dispossessed. Yet only a half-century earlier Colonel John Graham had been leading his brand-new Cape Regiment on campaigns to burn all Caffre kraals and cultivated fields.

Viewed from our neurotically fearful twenty-first century, the rural Cape Colony seems like the Garden of Eden before that incident with an apple. From Cape Town Lucie and Sally set off with Choslullah, their Malay driver, to follow rough mountain tracks through scattered villages. They stayed in 'publics' (not yet abbreviated to 'pubs') and Lucie often comments on the cleanliness of homes and persons. 'The Hottentots are far cleaner in their huts than any but the *very best* English poor . . . Fleas and bugs are not half so bad as in France.' Nobody locked their doors or kept watchdogs, never mind hiring security guards. At that date few English visitors ventured beyond Cape Town but to her mother Lucie explained, 'I like this inn-life, because I see all the "neighbours" – farmers and traders – whom I like far better than the *gentility* of Cape Town.'

One afternoon, at the hamlet of Palmiet River, 'We went into a neat little "public" and had porter and ham sandwiches, for which I paid 4s. & 6d. to a miserable-looking Englishwoman' – an exorbitant price. Hours later they came upon a mud cottage, half-farm, half-inn, where an ancient German couple served an excellent supper of chops and bread and butter. That meal, and a tiny dark bedroom and a good breakfast, 'cost ninepence for all'. Lucie invariably counted the pennies; she had to, hers was a journey undertaken cheerfully on a shoe-string. In such lodgings, this non-memsahib was content to sleep on mattresses of maize straw and to 'tub' in what little muddy water might be available. She reproved herself for occasionally being extravagant enough to drink good claret – when the alternatives were '"New Wine" at a penny a glass, enough to blow your head off, and "Cape Smoke" (brandy, like vitriol) at ninepence a bottle'.

Lucie lingered for a fortnight at Caledon where the octogenarian bachelor postman Heer Klein and his friend Heer Ley 'became great cronies of mine'. Heer Klein recalled that many young slaves had prospered, when freed, and then been kind to those of their former owners who had fallen on hard times. Lucie particularly relished her crony's personal reminiscences. Rosina, one of his slave-girls ('handsome, clever, the best horse-breaker, bullock-trainer and driver in the district'), bore him two children, then had 'six by another white man, and a few more by two husbands of her own race!' In middle age she took to the bottle and, after emancipation in 1834, celebrated every anniversary of that event by standing outside Heer Klein's window while loudly reading the statute.

The Malays soon became Lady Duff Gordon's favourite Cape inhabitants and back among the 'gentility' she raised many English eyebrows by frequently accepting Malay hospitality. The then fashionable form of Anglo-Islamophobia insisted that Mohammedans entertained Europeans only to poison them, so nobody expected an Englishwoman to pray one Friday in Cape Town's Chiappini Street mosque.

A fat jolly Mollah looked amazed as I ascended the steps; but when I touched my forehead and said, 'Salaam Aleikoom', he

laughed and said, 'Salaam, Salaam, come in, come in.' The
faithful poured in, leaving their wooden clogs in company with
my shoes . . . Women suckled their children and boys played as
I sat on the floor in a remote corner. The chanting was very fine
and the whole ceremony very decorous and solemn.

Returning to the mosque on the last evening of Ramadan, 'I
found myself supplied by one Mollah with a chair, and by another
with a cup of tea . . . They spoke English very little but made up for
it by their usual good breeding and intelligence.' No doubt they had
observed their guest's failure to censure those penniless English emigrant girls who turned 'Malay' and professed Islam, 'getting thereby
husbands who know not billiards and brandy . . . They risk a plural-
ity of wives but get fine clothes and industrious husbands.' Lucie had
recently been warned not to visit Muslims by a clergyman's widow
whose husband had gone mad three years after accepting a cup of
coffee from a Malay. Scornfully she noted, 'It is exactly like the
medieval feeling about the Jews.'

Predictably, Lucie warmed to the Cape's 'very pleasant Jews'.
Mr L. bred pigs on his model farm yet claimed to be 'a thorough
Jew in faith' while choosing to say his prayers in English and not to
'dress himself up in a veil and phylacteries'. He and his wife spoke
of England as 'home' and cared no more than their neighbours
for Jerusalem. But 'They have not forgotten the old persecutions,
and are civil to the coloured people, and speak of them in quite a
different tone from other English colonists.'

While awaiting a suitable homebound ship (a weary six-week wait,
costing 'no end of money and temper'), Lucie was both exasperated
and diverted by Christian denominational infighting. On 4 April she
observed, 'There is still altogether a nice kettle of religious hatred
brewing here.' The Anglican Bishop of Cape Town saw himself as
'absolute monarch of all he surveys'. His chaplain had recently told a
Mrs J. not to hope for salvation in the Dutch church, whose clergy

had not been ordained – hence their administration of the sacraments could only lead 'unto damnation'. An Admiral and his family were being anathematized for attending a bazaar in aid of the Wesleyan chapel, while an Irish maid at the Caledon Inn had been provoked by her bishop's intolerance into marrying at the Lutheran church.

By 16 May the good ship *Camperdown* had been a week at sea and Lucie was enjoying hundreds of frisking porpoises 'glittering green and bronze in the sun'. Ten days later, near St Helena, 'a large shark paid us a visit . . . a beautiful fish in shape and very graceful in motion . . . Last week we saw a young whale, a baby, about thirty feet long, and had a good view of him as he played around the ship'. This final letter held a warning: 'I hope you won't expect too much in the way of improvement in my health.'

Too soon, Lucie again had to flee the English climate. This time she settled in Luxor, perfected her Arabic and endeared herself to all her neighbours, especially the poor, the maimed and the exploited. During the next few years she made a close study of rural manners and customs and wrote her celebrated *Letters from Egypt*. In 1869 she died, was buried in Cairo's English cemetery and was mourned for the rest of the century (and longer) by her many Egyptian friends. They referred to her as 'the beautiful lady who was just and had a heart that loved Arabs'.

DERVLA MURPHY was born in Co. Waterford in 1931 where she still lives. Since 1963 she has been travelling by bicycle or on foot (usually beyond Europe) and returning to Lismore to write about her experiences. Her latest book, *A Month by the Sea: Encounters in Gaza*, was published by Eland in February.

Black Dogs and Stone Pianos

ANTHONY LONGDEN

Despite the solidity of its dry stone walls and its rugged beauty, the landscape of the Yorkshire Dales is fragile. By the 1920s, more vulnerable still was the way of life that had continued there for hundreds of years but which was rapidly dying out. Two young women – the writer Ella Pontefract and the artist Marie Hartley – realized that if no record were kept, more than a thousand years of rural tradition would vanish without trace. They decided to do something about it, and embarked on a remarkable literary enterprise that continues to illuminate the life and lore of the Dales. The collaboration was also to bring the companions domestic fulfilment and, to their surprise, a whiff of celebrity.

They produced many books, but I am especially fond of two in particular – *Yorkshire Cottage* (1942) and *Yorkshire Heritage* (1950). The first, produced on that wartime paper that now feels so soft to the touch, rather like velvet, paints a vivid picture of the women's work restoring an ancient cottage. The second is a poignant memoir.

Though Ella and Marie were Yorkshirewomen, they were not native to the Dales. They met in the West Riding in the mid-1920s when Ella, born of wealthy textile manufacturing and yeoman farmer

Ella Pontefract and Marie Hartley, *Swaledale* (1934), *Wensleydale* (1936), *The Charm of Yorkshire Churches* (1936), *Wharfedale* (1938), *Yorkshire Tour* (1939) and *Yorkshire Cottage* (1942), are all out of print, as is Marie Hartley's *Yorkshire Heritage: A Memoir to Ella Pontefract* (1950).

stock, was 27 and Marie, whose family were prosperous wool merchants, was 18. In *Yorkshire Heritage*, Marie recalls:

It was pure coincidence when in 1925 the Pontefracts built a house at Wetherby, a field's length away from the one that my family had moved into two years previously. The beginning of our acquaintance was not propitious; for the new house spoilt our view of the lower foothills of Wharfedale, on the edge of the Plain of York. But, instead of the bitterness that could so easily have developed, the families had too many similarities and interests in common to disagree, and they eventually established a firm friendship that never waned throughout the years that followed.

The women made frequent trips to the Dales, at a time when such excursions were not considered a becoming activity for young ladies.

When we went on our walking tours the word hiker had not been coined, nor were bizarre clothes at all a familiar sight in public places. I remember returning from Wharfedale and changing trains at Shipley where a crowd of mill girls following us along the platform jeered at our oddly-garbed figures in shabby tweed skirts, cloche hats shrunk by rain and resembling the headgear of a village idiot in a Phillpotts play, bulging rucksacks, and nailed shoes.

When Marie won a place to study art at the Slade School in London in 1931, Ella followed her, attending classes at University College and taking private tuition in journalism. On their return to Yorkshire, the pair started to work together and in 1932 the *Yorkshire Weekly Post* began to publish their series of illustrated articles 'The Charm of Yorkshire Churches', which ran for over three years. The Hartley-Pontefract partnership soon attracted the attention of a publisher and five Dales books followed, based on their research.

They had realized the importance of preserving humble, everyday domestic items of the kind which so easily slip away unnoticed. To that end they attended a punishing round of markets, auctions and house sales, recording everything they bought in meticulous detail – an oatcake rack, perhaps, or clogging irons used for shaping the wooden soles of clogs, or a flake on which hams and bacon were dried. On one occasion, they walked away from a sale weighed down by a packhorse collar with seven bells, three knitting sheaths, a copper ale-warmer, a tinderbox, a cattle horn and a jug from a Wesleyan chapel in Leyburn used at 'love feasts' in the nineteenth century.

Accompanied by Marie's distinctive illustrations, these Dales volumes also give a voice to vivid characters. Neddy Dick was a resourceful musician of great local acclaim. 'No visitor to the dale in his day failed to call on Neddy Dick, famous for his stone piano made from boulders picked out of the bed of the Swale, and his harmonium with its set of bells collected from clocks up and down the dale. These latter he played with a stick held in his left hand, and while striking the bass note with the butt, he tapped a bell with the other part of the stick, and played a mouth-organ at the same time.'

Then there was old Jane Ryder, a fount of folklore, with tales of black dogs 'with eyes like saucers' and other apparitions dating back to the first Viking settlers. It was Mrs Ryder who sent them a verse called 'Time is Money', which might otherwise have been lost:

> We need a year to grow a pig
> And two before a steer is big.
> The hens lay every day.
>
> A field of grain but once we reap
> A yearly fleece take off the sheep.
> The hens lay every day.
>
> A few short months the honey store
> The blossom fruit and all is o'er.
> The hens lay every day.

For other things too long we wait
And life is short and pay day late.
The hens lay every day.

In the early days of the project, money was tight, and their frequent fact-finding tours proved a drain on their meagre resources. To ease the financial pain Ella and Marie bought a Winchester caravan, 'Green Plover', which they towed with an Alvis or Austin. Friendly farmers allowed them to park the caravan in their fields, and the vehicle became their base until the day when an elderly friend in Askrigg, John Lodge, told them that Coleshouse, a cottage dating back to 1699, was for sale in the village.

The pull of a cottage in Wensleydale was irresistible, but they wanted to do things properly. As Ella wrote, 'A great responsibility

rests on anyone who alters an old building. If you erect an unlovely house your neighbours and the passers-by have to bear its ugliness; but the onus is on you; and future generations may, with a clear conscience, raze it to the ground. But if you destroy or mar an old building you deprive future generations of part of their heritage.'

There followed the trials and tribulations of knocking an ancient place into habitable shape. The women's account of this period was to be *Yorkshire Cottage* which, despite being published in wartime and therefore in limited numbers, was still a success. Here, Ella's prose transports you to the cosy hearth that was the women's haven against the elements outside:

We have hung our dripping mackintoshes to dry, and shaken off our gum boots. It was splendid out there in the rain hearing the thunder of the becks and the groaning of the trees; but now it is good to shut the storm out with the night. Draw the curtains, pull the chairs up to the fire, pile on another log. Let the wind roar as it will, the strong stone walls of the cottage will protect us. What were those words of the mason as he finished the job? 'There, it's done. And it'll be standing firm a thousand years from now.' A vain boast? You would not think so if you had seen the walls being built. There is nothing sham about them. Where they look two feet thick they are two feet thick, where they appear to be stone they are stone, not thin facings of it over brick as in much suburban building.

Yorkshire Cottage brought unexpected fame. Marie later recalled ruefully: 'In the book we avoided giving away the name of the village . . . and in our innocence we never thought that, apart perhaps from local people, anyone would take the trouble to ascertain its whereabouts. We were sadly mistaken, and that summer we learnt what fame meant.' Fans of the book dropped in on them morning, noon and night, and letters arrived from soldiers in the Middle East and India, and from prisoners-of-war in Germany who had managed to get hold of *Yorkshire Cottage* from camp libraries.

Ella's health had always been fragile, but by 1943 it had deteriorated to the stage where there was little chance of recovery. She died on 23 February 1945, at the age of 49, leaving Marie devastated. It was another five years before she was able to write *Yorkshire Heritage*, 'a tribute to Ella Pontefract'. She concludes it by reflecting on the redemptive power of writing.

For myself it is enough to say that from the world that had crashed about me, the only salvage seemed to be the diaries that I had kept during the years of Ella's and my joyous work together in the dales. In time I began to see a purpose in life, and eventually took up the writing of this book.

Marie Hartley's own story ended quite differently. The work she began with Ella was continued with the women's mutual friend, the writer Joan Ingilby, and the final tally of Dales titles stood at forty. The books co-authored by Ingilby are detailed, quite scholarly works, and can still be found in second-hand bookshops across the land, particularly in the north, of course. But for me, they somehow lack the warmth and charm of *Yorkshire Cottage* and those first Dales books.

By the early 1970s, the Askrigg cottage was so full of artefacts that Marie and Joan felt compelled to donate them to the local council, and they eventually formed the basis of the collection at the Dales Countryside Museum at Hawes. Marie and Joan were made MBEs for their contribution to recording the Dales' history and received honorary degrees from the Open University. Joan died in 2000, aged 89, but Marie worked on in Askrigg for another six years, dying there at the age of 100 just after passing the proofs of a short biography, *The Harvest of a Quiet Eye*, written to mark her centenary.

ANTHONY LONGDEN loves nothing better than haunting the stacks of the London Library and discovering things he never went looking for in the first place. The rest of the time he is a journalist, press complaints commissioner and media consultant.

Ella and Marie's companions

A Lost Generation

TONY ROBERTS

Many years ago my wife and I were confined by the police to our hot hotel in Rhodes for an evening, a fate we shared with other tourists as a result of anticipated demonstrations against the appearance of a Turkish ship in the harbour. It was another time of strained relations between Greeks and Turks. Up in our room, I decided it was time I asserted myself as a war correspondent. Out on the balcony with notepad and pen, I could hear the anger and the pounding feet below. I began to scribble – then heard the launching of canisters, smelled the tear gas and nimbly stepped back into our room, all my bravado gone. I picked up the Hemingway I had been reading and poured myself another glass of retsina. He can take you that way.

Now, thirty years later, I have just reread Ernest Hemingway's first and best novel, *The Sun also Rises*, written when he and the century were 26 years old. It is a *roman à clef*, dispensing justice and injustice to members of the Parisian circle surrounding Hemingway and his first wife, Hadley. One of the novel's epigraphs is the now famous remark Gertrude Stein seized upon, 'You are all a lost generation.' In fact, 'wasted' might be a better adjective to describe a novel in which a bunch of literary drunks gather round a nymphomaniac at Parisian café tables, before taking off for the Spanish bullfights in Pamplona, where each earns his horns. Yet what I loved about the novel – and, with a little more tolerance for human weakness produced by the passing years, still do – is its mixture of post-war

Ernest Hemingway, *The Sun also Rises* (first published in Britain as *Fiesta*: 1926)
Arrow · Pb · 224pp · £7.99 · ISBN 9780099908500

pessimism and gaiety, fuelled by constant drinking and banter.

First though, with Hemingway there is always the man to get past in order to see the print up close, a man whose life was made up of large appetites and a shoal of little fictions. Hemingway (1899–1961) came out of a Chicago suburb and, imaginatively, the woods of northern Michigan. After serving as an ambulance driver in the First World War on the Italian front, where he was wounded, he became a newspaper man in Paris, then a stylistically innovative author. Later incarnations included war correspondent, big-game hunter, deep-sea fisherman and world-class celebrity.

He left behind him bestsellers, a Nobel Prize, four marriages and their resulting children. There is an enormous difference between the uncomplicated Hemingway heroes and the man himself, whose turbulent life ended in suicide at the age of 62. Like John Wayne, in the popular imagination Hemingway increasingly *became* his code, though its macho element does not always sit well with today's attitudes. (There is a highly entertaining parody of the man and his famous 'grace under pressure' in Woody Allen's film *Midnight in Paris*.)

The idea of Paris in the 1920s is formidably attractive to the romantic sensibility. For American bohemians of the day it offered artistic licence, sexual freedom, the absence of Prohibition and an admirable exchange rate – so much so that by 1924 thirty thousand Americans were living there permanently. Hemingway was one of the early beneficiaries, writing for the Toronto *Star* and living on his earnings and his wife's trust fund. His prose captured the character of the left bank's Latin Quarter. 'The Dôme', 'The Select', 'The Rotonde' were in full swing – cafés with their zinc bars, the little saucers piling up after each Pernod, the artists and their models, the *poules*, the *bal-musette* music, the *bateaux mouches* on the Seine.

The greater part of *The Sun also Rises*, however, takes place in Spain, where the characters attend the San Fermin bullfighting festival in Pamplona, at the foot of the Pyrenees. Events are spun from the misadventures of the Hemingways and their friends on a trip in

June 1925. The narrator Jake Barnes (unlike the author) is fluent in French and Spanish, which leads to innumerable incidental encounters that add flavour to the book. At the Spanish frontier, for example, Jake talks to a carabineer about a man refused passage:

> 'What's the matter with the old one?' I asked.
> 'He hasn't got any passport.'
> I offered the guard a cigarette. He took it and thanked me.
> 'What will he do?' I asked.
> The guard spat in the dust.
> 'Oh, he'll just wade across the stream.'

Their trip begins peacefully enough, with Jake and his writer friend Bill Gorton fishing in northern Spain. On the way we meet Hemingway's peasants: noble, curious and bibulous figures, eager to share their wineskins. They have the simple dignity Hemingway afforded his working men. He has a wonderful ear for their dialogue, with its quiet, courtly humour. Later things get rowdier, when the rest of the gang descend on Pamplona and its bulls.

Oddly, given that the novel's central character is a newspaperman in this turbulent post-war period, we have no sense of contemporary events. What is implied of the European economic collapse comes from references to the exchange rate and an obsession with money. According to the Hemingway authority Scott Donaldson, money is central to the moral code of the novel: you have to pay for what you get in life. Those who earn their money, like Jake and Bill, are to be trusted. Those who are improvident, like Lady Brett Ashley, the novel's *femme fatale*, are not.

Although all the men are attracted to Brett, the novel's true magnet is Hemingway's alter ego Jake. He is a man who is trusted, even loved, by all. As his friend Bill Gorton says, 'You're a hell of a good guy.' Jake is as attractively sour as Clark Gable's newspaperman in *It Happened One Night* (1934), and as observant and passive as that other great Jazz Age narrator Nick Carraway in F. Scott Fitzgerald's

The Great Gatsby (1925). A war wound has literally emasculated him, eternally frustrating his relationship with the lovely, alcoholic Brett. Nevertheless his passion for her is undiminished, as is his enthusiasm for the 'manly sports' of drinking, fishing and bullfighting.

If Jake is the moral compass of the novel, Brett Ashley is its magnetic storm. Another character, Robert Cohn, calls her Circe, since she has men behaving like swine. Brett is chronically unreliable, but enchanting, independent and tough. Jake tries to shield her from the blood of the gored steers, but she enjoys seeing how the bulls work, shifting horns like boxers. In public she is a delicious drunk. In private she is a pitiable figure, confessing to Jake at one point, 'I've never been able to help anything.' She seduces the young bullfighter, 'the Romero Boy', and claims she has lost her self-respect as a result. However, she finally lets the bullfighter

Anna Trench

go, explaining to Jake, 'You know it makes me feel rather good deciding not to be a bitch.'

Other characters contribute to the gaiety. The two war veterans Bill Gorton and Mike Campbell, the latter a Scots bankrupt and nominally the wayward Brett's fiancé, are both drunks. There is much humour in their dialogue, as when Bill declares that stuffed animals are needed to brighten up a place:

> See that horse-cab? Going to have that horse-cab stuffed for you for Christmas. Going to give all my friends stuffed animals. I'm a nature writer.

Balancing this, much of the pain in the novel comes from the treatment of Cohn, a wealthy Jewish writer (who has boxed but not seen war). Everyone takes a turn at being contemptuous of Cohn.

His sin is his jealous obsession with Brett. The native characters show more self-restraint and are rendered charming by the formality of their English, particularly Romero the handsome young bullfighter and the Greek Count Mippipopolous, both conquests of Brett's.

Hemingway's spare, modernist, 'hard-boiled' style has been as easy to parody as the author himself. It is artfully simple, repetitive, uncluttered, fond of conjunctions and distrustful of adjectives. It is a style difficult to get right convincingly, even for Hemingway (eventually it became a mannered affair, tipping toward self-parody). However, *The Sun also Rises* is superbly done, concise and credible. It is also vividly convincing, because Hemingway had learnt the trick of realism early. So for example, Jake apologizes part way into the novel for not getting a character right: 'Somehow I feel I have not shown Robert Cohn clearly.' It is a device that allows us to see Jake as an open-minded fellow.

The truth is that showing a thing clearly and therefore achieving the sense of being there is the great strength of Hemingway as a writer. We see it in *The Sun also Rises* in its artful simplicity:

> In the morning it was bright and they were sprinkling the streets of the town and we all had breakfast in a café. Bayonne is a nice town. It is like a very clean Spanish town and it is on a big river. Already, so early in the morning, it was very hot on the bridge across the river. We walked out on the bridge and then took a walk through the town.

Throughout his writing career, according to Michael Reynolds in his fascinating *Hemingway: The Paris Years*, he gave his readers 'what he later called "the way it was": the people, the weather, the look and feel of a place, the small detail capturing on paper the intense moment forever fresh'. The point, as Hemingway himself explained, was to 'write one true sentence, and then go on from there'.

The Sun also Rises is admittedly not to everyone's taste. The casual, repetitive anti-Semitism is off-putting: critics have built careers on exploring the issue, as they have with other accusations, of misogyny and homophobia. Bullfighting, too, is deservedly anathema to most of us today.

But if one can side-step all that and see the book as of its time, *The Sun also Rises* is a fine and often hilarious novel with an infectious style. As the trailer for the 1957 Tyrone Power-Ava Gardner film version had it: 'The Sun Never Rose on a Bolder Hemingway Story!' If you haven't read it you should treat yourself. As Nick Adams, his other alter ego, would say, 'It's a swell book.' It may have you swaggering just like Hemingway – at least until the first whiff of tear gas.

TONY ROBERTS was educated in England and America. After 30 years teaching – an occupation not unlike that of war correspondent – he turned to writing poetry, reviews and essays. His third collection of poems, *Outsiders*, is published by Shoestring Press.

Persia on Exmoor

CYNTHIA CLINCH

I have never been on horseback. The best I can offer is a snap of myself, captioned 'September 1937, Littlehampton'. Aged $3\frac{1}{2}$, hair in bunches, apprehension in eyes, I am installed on the back of a donkey with the sea as a backdrop.

The photograph in question fell out of a recently rediscovered book, *The Far-Distant Oxus*, in which horses – or rather ponies – play the leading role. The date of publication is 1937, the very year of the snap, though I am fairly sure that the book itself did not reach my hands until ten years later. Did I buy it myself with a Christmas or birthday book-token after foraging through the shelves of Bredon's bookshop in Brighton? Or did a clever aunt send it to me? I don't remember and it doesn't matter. What I can still recall is how I fell in love with it – with the dust jacket, the line drawings and the subject: ponies, Exmoor and children. I was totally ignorant of the first two but reckoned I did know something about the third.

The Far-Distant Oxus is a story of adventures: six children with six ponies, tales of camping, rafting, building their own hut, enjoying a freedom from parental watchfulness that amazed me even then. And, perhaps best of all, it was written by two girls, clever boarding-school girls, Katharine Hull and Pamela Whitlock. Together they wrote the twenty-three chapters, adding bold pen-and-ink illustrations and maps, all drawn by Pamela. The final draft was bravely sent off to Arthur Ransome, whose own books were clearly an inspiration (boats

Katharine Hull and Pamela Whitlock, *The Far-Distant Oxus* (1937)
Fidra Books · Pb · £12 · ISBN 9781906123147

in his case, not ponies), and he in turn sent it to his publisher Jonathan Cape, who read it, loved it and immediately published it. I dreamed of writing like that, and then forgot about it.

Until 1974. By this time I was part-owner of an Arab dhow in Abu Dhabi, still had not attempted horse-riding, but was at least writing a weekly column for the local English-language newspaper. This explains why I found myself lurking on the fringes of an expatriate reception one evening, looking for material. The material found me – Helen, a sixth-generation Australian, brought up in Melbourne, with no exposure to horses, but a greedy reader of books of all kinds.

How did we establish that, at the age of 12 and separated by more than 10,000 miles, we had both read and loved *The Far-Distant Oxus* and could still remember its plot? By the time we did so we must have covered a great deal of conversational ground, not all of it to do with books.

One thing we certainly didn't discuss was the book's title, nor the quotations prefacing each chapter. Their source is in fact revealed in the text, but Matthew Arnold's poem *Sohrab and Rustum* meant nothing to me at the age of 12 and still didn't thirty years later, when I actually went to live in Iran. I had forgotten that those clever girls had culled from Arnold's poem versions of his Persian place-names to disguise those of their beloved Exmoor landscape: Aderbijan, Siestan, Mount Elbruz, Organje, the Aral Sea – names and places that were to become familiar to me. But the book itself was not lost, just straying, packed carelessly at the bottom of a travelling trunk.

It is only now on rereading it that I find myself playing the detective. How was it possible for six children to live in such freedom, far from adult control? Where were the parents? There is a reference to 'coming home from Sumatra' and of the sea being 'as far away as Africa . . . as far away as Mummy and Daddy'. Three of the children lodge with the local farmer and his wife, who hire them ponies and do puzzled duty as their guardians; two others have an indulgent father ('Daddy doesn't mind what we do') living in a fine house on

Exmoor where he tends his roses and from which he usefully absents himself to London for as long as a week at a time – no sign of a mother. And in the case of the sixth and most charismatic member of the group, young Maurice, no home or adult appears in his life at any point. He does, however, have a black labrador, Ellita ('the Persian for dragon', he claims), a dashing pony, a sleeping-bag and mysterious supplies of money. In short, he's a dark-haired romantic figure, though he's only 14. I assume that the two authors were already in love with Heathcliff and Darcy, of whom I then knew nothing.

It is Maurice who becomes the mastermind of their adventures. From concealed resources he provides building materials for their hut, food for campfires, money for sausages from the local shop. All their small adventures – sleeping on haystacks, riding moorland trails, saving a mare and foal from an Exmoor round-up, winning a pig at a fête – are training for the big idea: a three-day expedition down the River Oxus to the Aral Sea.

So they build a raft. Then they stock it, cunningly get adult permission, and set off with six ponies, taking turns to ride or to pole their craft along. There are setbacks, of course – shallow waters, mist, detours, errors. Until '"The sea! The sea!" Bridget cried ecstatically.'

Pouring rain, wet matches, a lack of food on the way back, nothing detracts from that great moment. Spirits only sag when the holiday ends. But Maurice plays a final card. With dry matches he lights four farewell beacons across the moors before wordlessly riding off into the night. '"He's gone", said Frances.'

It was Maurice who first made my heart beat. Another enduring influence on my tastes was Pamela Whitlock's illustrations. I loved her two maps, especially the one which traces the journey of their self-built raft. And then there are lists. The children write a list of expeditionary essentials which opens with six hammocks and runs through thirty items, ending with dog biscuits and saddle dusters. I realize now that it is to *The Far-Distant Oxus* that I owe my own irritating obsession with lists, for shopping, cooking, reading, travelling.

I suspect that if I were 13 today, preparing for a trip down the Oxus on a raft, my list would begin and end with a mobile phone. Times have changed. Still, if you are lucky enough to have young teenagers in your life who love ponies and long for adventure, give them a copy of *The Far-Distant Oxus* and ask in return for their own list of essentials required on such a trip. But first of all, before handing it over, read it yourself and travel back in time to the freedom of those prelapsarian, pre-Second World War years. Oh, and read *Sohrab and Rustum* as well – preferably out loud. It's stirring stuff.

CYNTHIA CLINCH has still never been on horseback nor built a raft, but she has successfully swapped the River Oxus for the Cam in Cambridge, with its punt-infested waters beside which only cows graze.

Certainly not Cricket

JEREMY LEWIS

Military men write better prose than most – by the nature of their work they eschew ambiguity and long-windedness in favour of plain-speaking – and Christie Lawrence was no exception to the rule. 'We were very tired of Crete' runs the opening sentence of *Irregular Adventure*, which was published by Faber in 1947 and is one of the neglected masterpieces of the Second World War.

As a 24-year-old captain in Robert Laycock's No. 8 Commando, Lawrence was caught up in the chaos that followed the German invasion of Crete in May 1941, when British troops were forced to evacuate the island; and although his book describes his subsequent adventures fighting with the Chetniks in German-occupied Yugoslavia, Crete is its point of departure.

According to his fellow-officer Evelyn Waugh, all those serving in No. 8 Commando were 'highly individualistic' characters who had volunteered because they sought service more adventurous than was offered at the time by normal regimental life. 'No one could ask for a better thriller,' Waugh declared in his introduction to *Irregular Adventure*: Lawrence's exploits 'should bring encouragement to all who may be in danger of doubting whether knight-errantry is still possible in the conditions of modern war'. Six years earlier, in the shambolic retreat to the south coast of Crete, Waugh caught a last glimpse of Lawrence in a cave near Sphakia. 'He or I or both of us were slightly delirious,' he recalled. 'I remember his telling me a rambling story of his having run into a rock on a motor-bicycle. Then

---

Christie Lawrence, *Irregular Adventure* (1947), is out of print.

carrying two rifles he wandered off again, alone, in the direction of the enemy.'

Whereas Waugh made his way back to Cairo, Lawrence was captured by the Germans and sent, via Athens, to Salonika for the long train journey north to a prisoner-of-war camp in Germany. Life for British prisoners-of-war was a good deal harder than one imagines, and food was in short supply. 'It is a shock to see Englishmen, educated at the world's most famous universities, scavenging for potato peelings,' Lawrence writes, adding that 'the greatest shock is when you find yourself scavenging with them'. A former journalist who – rather inconveniently, as it turned out – wore large horn-rimmed specs, Lawrence was intrepid, ingenious and determined to escape. Earlier attempts had come to nothing, but as the cattle-trucks trundled slowly through Serbia, he managed to force open a barred window and leapt out.

After the dust and dryness of Greece, Serbia seemed like a paradise, overflowing with plums for the eating, and mulberry trees, and fields of maize in which to hide when danger threatened, and mustachioed men in waistcoats who needed no excuse to hand out glasses of raki. Lawrence was overwhelmed by the 'boundless hospitality' of the Serbian peasants, but he was determined to make his way to Turkey, a neutral country, and he set off for northern Greece and the Turkish border. Within spitting distance of Turkey he was captured by Bulgarian soldiers, and was back in a train heading north. Once again he made his escape – only to find himself back in Serbia, not far from where he had started out.

Serbia in high summer may have seemed idyllic, but Lawrence soon realized that the fighting in Yugoslavia was an unusually brutal affair, made worse by the fact that it was as much a civil war as a war against the Germans. The right-wing Chetniks, led by Dražha Mihailovich, were supported, for the time being at least, by the British, but the scale and the savagery of German reprisals made them increasingly reluctant to take action against the occupying forces; nor were they prepared to co-operate with the altogether more ruthless partisans, communist guerrillas who were supported by Russia after the Soviet Union entered the war in June 1941. And, to complicate matters further, a group of Chetniks led by Kosta Pechanats were actively collaborating with the Germans, fighting both the partisans and Mihailovich's forces.

Later in the war, Churchill switched his support from Mihailovich to the partisans on the recommendation of Fitzroy Maclean and Bill Deakin, who felt that Tito was far more committed to fighting the Germans, and after the war the hapless Chetnik leader was shot on a golf course outside Belgrade. In the meantime, Christie Lawrence – 'Krsta Lorents' to his new comrades-in-arms – spent a year fighting with Mihailovich's Chetniks. He 'tried not to flinch' when a heavily bearded guerrilla leader seized him in a bear-like embrace, and kissed him on the lips. He taught himself Serbo-Croat, and was soon involved in ambushing enemy convoys, blowing up bridges and acting as an intermediary between various factions, some of whom were more interested in fighting each other than the enemy.

Winter was coming on, and life in the snow-covered mountains was almost unendurable: he lost one of his boots in an enemy attack, and incurred frostbite as he hobbled about the hillsides with a heavily bandaged foot; posing as a Slovenian, he made his way into war-torn towns and villages to meet up with fellow-resisters, rubbing shoulders with collaborators and German soldiers in bars and cafés; a touch of romance was provided by Danielle, a dashing Jewish girl who performed wonders with a machine-gun: she is killed in action and Lawrence is soundly berated for dragging her body back to be buried while leaving her precious machine-gun behind.

But in the end his luck ran out: captured once again by the Germans, 'I had that slightly sick feeling you get when you are first in to bat, only worse.' The last three sentences of *Irregular Adventure* are as laconic as its opening. He had been put in a windowless cell and chained to his bunk by a black-clad SS man clutching a tommy-gun. 'He went outside and shut the door. Then the light went out. And I knew that I was in the hands of the Gestapo.'

Two years after the war had ended, in November 1947, Evelyn Waugh had lunch with Christie Lawrence. 'His circumstances are not easy, with a wife and child, no house but lodgings,' Waugh noted in his diary, adding that 'his health and sanity are enfeebled by Gestapo torture'. He had earned £180 from sales of *Irregular Adventure*, but although the reviews had been good, there were no plans for a second impression. He was keen to join the colonial service, ideally in Uganda. Waugh offered him financial help if he stayed in England, but nothing came of that: a month later Waugh saw his army friend Basil Bennett and reported that 'he has given Chris Lawrence £300 and had a sharp note in reply. Why?'

'The end of this book raises the hope that there will be a sequel,' Waugh wrote in his introduction to *Irregular Adventure*, but none was forthcoming. Christie Lawrence is not mentioned by any of Waugh's biographers, and his book has – like its creator – vanished into oblivion. Trawling through David Astor's papers, I came across one mention – no more – of a 'Christie Lawrence' in Northern Rhodesia, and the British Library Catalogue lists alongside his wartime memoir a book called *Mary Goes to School*, published in Lusaka in 1960 by the Northern Information Department. One longs to know what happened to this remarkable if tormented man.

It used to be claimed that the Second World War produced little lasting literature when compared with the First. Yet the memoirs in particular are often outstanding, and many of the best – Fitzroy Maclean's *Eastern Approaches*, David Smiley's *Albanian Assignment*, Julian Amery's *Sons of the Eagle* – are set in the Balkans. *Irregular Adventure* is a wonderful piece of work, and deserves to be better remembered.

JEREMY LEWIS's most recent book, *Shades of Greene: One Generation of an English Family*, is now available in paperback. He is researching a biography of David Astor, the former editor of the *Observer*, to be published by Jonathan Cape.

Hawking the Owls

TESSA WEST

Anna Trench

Open any magazine whose readers include novice or would-be writers – from *Writers' News* to the *London Review of Books* to *Mslexia* – and it's clear that there must be an increasing number of people prepared to pay to be published. There are numerous businesses which say they will turn your manuscript into a real book, and they probably do a decent job. But the real issue for a self-publisher, whether this is someone who does it virtually on their own as I do, or a company with a sales team, is marketing.

Having sold some thousands of my first two self-published novels and made a profit (as long as I don't factor in actual writing time), I decided to devote a day to selling my third. My novels are all set in East Anglia and it's this geographical aspect that enables me to interest the local media, big and small booksellers, and a range of other less conventional outlets such as museums, tearooms and pubs. I've learned that it's well worth the trouble to seek out the last group. One pub, featured in my first novel, sold 200 copies. Moreover, the landlord agreed to a 25 per cent discount – a much more generous deal than any bookshop gave. Better still, I never had to send invoices or

Tessa West's three novels are published under the imprint Fox Books in paperback at £7.99 each: *Companion to Owls* (2008) · 258pp · ISBN 9780954362720; *The Estuary* (2002) · 286pp · ISBN 9780954362706; *The Reed Flute* (2004) · 212pp · ISBN 9780954362713. *The Curious Mr Howard* (2011) is published by the Waterside Press (Pb · 384pp · £29.95 · ISBN 9781904380733).

chase them up. I'd just turn up at the pub when they wanted another pack of books and the landlord would reach for the beer mug containing my takings, insist I count the cash there and then, and pour me a half of Adnams.

Few bookshops buy and re-order self-published books without prompting, and even if they do you also have to get out there and sell them directly, which is why I spent one August Bank Holiday Saturday at Thorney, near Peterborough. I chose this small village because my novel *Companion to Owls* is set there. So, having arranged to have a stall at the tri-annual flower festival, I and my partner Ralph loaded a pile of the hot-off-the-press copies into my Mini and set off for the Fens.

It was a beautiful day and the Abbey Green was full of people sticking numbers on bottles, erecting gazebos and spreading cloths on trestle tables. It all seemed very English, especially when the vicar started things off with a prayer.

I very quickly realized that the spot I'd been allocated was not a good one because it was off the route which most people took as they ambled round in the first proper sunshine we'd had for weeks. We shifted our pitch to a better spot, but still didn't get much attention. Another tactic was required, so I picked up a couple of copies of the book and began to address passers-by.

My spiel was not very different from the one I use with book-buyers in shops. I'd say something like, 'Good morning. Can I interest you in this novel I've written?' As I held it out to them so they were likely to take hold of it, I added, 'It's set here – actually in Thorney.' The responses were legion, and as the day went on I became increasingly intrigued.

'I don't read. I'm a couch potato.'
'I don't live here. I live in Whittlesey, so it wouldn't mean anything to me.' (Whittlesey is just a few miles from Thorney.)
'I'm frightened of owls.'

'It's my wife who's the reader.'

Some people studied the cover intently, then the family tree at the beginning and the acknowledgements at the end. Then they'd begin to leaf through, only to return the book to me a few moments later. Some picked up one of my other novels and struggled to decide which to buy – and a few bought all three. I found myself reading the blurb aloud to people who had forgotten their glasses.

Others had no hesitation at all when I or Ralph approached them with our 'Could I interest you?' question.

'No. You can't.'

'Yes, of course. It looks great.'

Some were literally speechless and just shook their heads or looked at the ground, though a few tried to engage me in conversations on very different topics. It was impossible to predict how people would respond. Ralph and I made guesses based on stereotypes but this did not help at all. A bookish-looking couple (whatever that is) claimed only ever to read the local paper. When I approached a couple of 16-year-old lads one immediately bought a copy for his mother, borrowing the cash from his friend.

Money was certainly an issue. In order to avoid buying the book, some resorted to saying they had no money on them before heading off to invest in raffle tickets. And of course others would have liked to buy, but genuinely couldn't. I found myself urging them to order the book from the library. I was asked three times who the money was going to, and answered that, in common with the other stalls, 20 per cent was going to Thorney Abbey.

'I'd buy it but my husband/wife's got the money.'

'£7.99? Is it worth it?'

Once, towards the end of the day when I was beginning to weary a little, I was asked yet again what the book was about. As I explained, my listener started to fidget. So I stopped and asked, 'Not your sort of thing?'

'No. It's not for me.'

I couldn't help adding, 'So I've written the wrong book?'

'Yes.'

We watched the three tombolas do brisk business while the rows of jars on the home-made jam stall steadily diminished. We marvelled at the perennial interest in bric-à-brac.

'Who did you say wrote it? Oh, *you* did! Will you sign it for me?'

The sight of me signing always drew attention and I wondered later whether I might have sold more if I had just sat there all day writing. In the end I sold about fifty books, which felt quite respectable.

As we packed up someone said to my partner, 'Tessa West? Never heard of her, but I wish her well.'

Today I checked out the Saturday *Guardian*'s weekly best-seller chart. The paperback fiction list was headed by *One Day*. Like my book it costs £7.99, but it had sold 44,034 copies. Still, I bet David Nicholls didn't have as much fun as I did selling it. He certainly didn't consume as much tea and as many home-made scones, and he didn't even try to win a teddy bear.

TESSA WEST is the author of *The Estuary*, *The Reed Flute* and *Companion to Owls*. Waterside Press, which published her *Prisons of Promise* in 1997, has just brought out her biography of the prison reformer *The Curious Mr Howard*.

Bibliography

Sybille Bedford, *A Legacy*; *Quicksands: A Memoir*　　　　45

Artemis Cooper, *Patrick Leigh Fermor: An Adventure*　　　　23

Peter Dawson, *Fifty Years of Song*　　　　60

Patrick Leigh Fermor: *A Time of Gifts*; *Between the Woods and the Water*　　7

Michael Frayn, *The Russian Interpreter*　　　　55

Lady Duff Gordon, *Letters from the Cape*　　　　64

Marie Hartley, *Yorkshire Heritage: A Memoir to Ella Pontefract*　　　70

Ernest Hemingway, *The Sun also Rises*　　　　76

Richard Hillyer, *Country Boy*　　　　14

Katharine Hull and Pamela Whitlock, *The Far-Distant Oxus*　　　82

Michael Innes: the Inspector Appleby novels　　　　26

Maxine Hong Kingston, *The Woman Warrior: Memoirs of a Girlhood
among Ghosts*　　　　35

Christie Lawrence, *Irregular Adventure*　　　　86

Norman Lewis, *Naples '44*　　　　40

John Masters, *Nightrunners of Bengal*　　　　30

Ella Pontefract and Marie Hartley, *Swaledale*; *Wensleydale*; *The Charm
of Yorkshire Churches*; *Wharfedale*; *Yorkshire Tour*; *Yorkshire Cottage*　　70

J. D. Salinger, *Catcher in the Rye*　　　　20

Denton Welch, *Maiden Voyage*; *In Youth Is Pleasure*; *A Voice through a
Cloud*; *Journals*; *Where Nothing Sleeps: The Complete Short Stories
and Other Related Works*　　　　50

Tessa West: the novels of　　　　90

Slightly Foxed is expecting cubs!

Do you remember curling up with a children's book that transported you straight to some other time and place, that brought history to life in a way that school lessons didn't? If so, it could well have been written by the master storyteller Ronald Welch, author of an outstanding series of children's books which follow the fortunes of the Carey family from their involvement in the Crusades to service in the First World War.

William Stobbs

Unaccountably these marvellous novels, which together join up the dots of English history, have long been out of print. But now, we're delighted to announce that we'll be reissuing all 12 titles in a new and exciting series, Slightly Foxed Cubs.

Each title will be published with the original illustrations, in a limited and numbered edition of 2,000 copies, elegantly bound in cloth, and priced at £16 (UK), £18 (Europe) or £19 (Rest of the World), including p&p.

Scrupulously researched and true to life, they will, we feel, strike a nostalgic chord with older readers, and introduce a new generation of children to a writer who can make the stringing of a longbow and the precise armouring of a medieval knight equally fascinating. They've certainly had us gripped!

In September we'll be starting with three titles: *Knight Crusader*, winner of the Carnegie Medal in 1954, *For the King* and *The Galleon*. We'll be telling you more about these later.

If you would like to reserve a full set of these books, each with the same number, do let us know (all@foxedquarterly.com; tel 020 7033 0258). Some of the SFE titles are already fetching high prices on the Internet, so perhaps it's time to start collecting the new series now.

Coming attractions . . .

CHRISTOPHER RUSH exhibits true grit

DAISY HAY meets Jane Eyre

PENELOPE LIVELY returns to Alamein

ISABEL COLEGATE mourns Liberal England

HAZEL WOOD follows the Carey family

ROBIN KNIGHT hangs up his bat

AMANDA THEUNISSEN salutes a remarkable woman

ROGER JONES enjoys an Icelandic saga